The Modern Fox Terrier

By
Leonard E. Naylor

Vintage Dog Books
Home Farm
44 Evesham Road
Cookhill, Alcester
Warwickshire
B49 5LJ

www.vintagedogbooks.com

© Read Books 2005
This book is copyright and may not be
reproduced or copied in any way without
the express permission of the publisher in writing.

ISBN No. 1-905124-41-4

Published by Vintage Dog Books 2005
Vintage Dog books is an imprint of Read Books

British Library Cataloguing-in-Publication Data
A catalogue record for this book is available
from the British Library.

Vintage Dog Books
Home Farm
44 Evesham Road
Cookhill, Alcester
Warwickshire
B49 5LJ

THE MODERN FOX TERRIER

Mr. A. A. W. SIMMONDS'S EPPING EDITOR, BY Ch. TALAVERA SIMON OUT OF TALAVERA PATCHWORK. A BIG WINNER AT CHAMPIONSHIP SHOWS AND A SUCCESSFUL STUD DOG.

THE MODERN FOX TERRIER

TERRIER

ITS HISTORY, POINTS AND TRAINING

by

LEONARD E. NAYLOR

(Author of "The Irish Setter")

WITH PLATES

H. F. & G. WITHERBY

326 HIGH HOLBORN, LONDON, W.C.

First published 1933.

Printed for Messrs. H. F. & G. Witherby
at Middle Row Place, London.

CONTENTS

5

CONTENTS

8

LIST OF PLATES

9

To
M. V. N.

CHAPTER I

THE HISTORY AND EVOLUTION OF THE BREED

How the name arose—" Terriers " that are not—The ideal size—The " Wire's " English forebears—Terriers in the XVIth Century—The dawn of " Wire " history—" Parson Jack's " " Wires "—Caricaturist breeders—The breed's redemption—Some far-seeing experts—The Wire Fox Terrier Association.

THE word Terrier is derived from the Latin *terra*, or earth, and indicates clearly the sporting function of this type of dog. Many years have passed since the term Terrier was applied exclusively to dogs capable of going to ground, for some breeds that are included in the classification would have difficulty in getting more than their noses into an earth. The breeders of the Fox Terrier, however, throughout the years have borne the primary purpose of the breed in mind, and excessive size has always been regarded as a serious fault. Although the great majority of show-quality " Wires " have never explored the

11

THE MODERN FOX TERRIER

home of Brock the badger, they all approximate
to the ideal size for the job, and when put to it
would assuredly not be found wanting in other
respects. It is impossible to say when the " Wire "
was first evolved; in England there have been
Rough-Haired Terriers of various shades ever
since the appearance and uses of dogs began to
form the subject of pictorial and written record.
Certain it is that, at least a hundred and fifty
years ago, British engravers and draughtsmen
depicted small dogs, rough of coat and mainly
white in colour, which, allowing for artistic
licence and the passage of time, bear a distinct
family resemblance to our friend of to-day. It is
safe to assume that a Wire-Haired Terrier of sorts
has been in use ever since fox-hunting began.
Dr. Caius, in his sixteenth-century " Book of
Dogges ", refers to " Terrars " which " creepe into
the grounde, and by that means make afrayde,
nyppe and byte the badger, in such sorte, that
either they teare them in pieces with theyre teeth,
beying in the bosom of the earth, or else hayle
and pull them perforce out of theyre lurking
angles, dark dongeons, and close caves ".   The

worthy Doctor's idea of a badger-dig bears all the evidence of having been acquired at third-hand, like much of the rest of his dog-lore. (Of another breed he affirmed that they had the pretty conceit of waiting by rabbit-holes while the occupants were absent, posing as " friends ", and by this early form of the " confidence trick " waylaying the rodents upon their return !) But in any event the sixteenth-century Terrier, allowing for Dr. Caius's over-emphasis, was obviously a great fellow.

However, coming to the dawn of authentic " Wire " history we find, about the time of Queen Victoria's accession, that Wire-Haired Terriers in the north of England were quite plentiful, and it is recorded that the pedigrees of some of those strains were just as carefully kept as those of the leading kennels of to-day. In the south the Rev. John Russell (" Parson Jack ") had founded a kennel of " Wires " whose reputation had spread far beyond his native Devon. Many stories are told of the prowess of the " Wire " in the 'forties and 'fifties before dog-shows came into being, but we are very much in the dark regarding his precise physical make-up. Early in his show career the " improvers " got to work, for in the 'seventies of last century we find the Fox Terrier's body compared to a brick with the four corners knocked off. From this exaggerated cobbiness the pendulum swung to the other extreme, and the caricaturist breeders, under the pretence of further " improvement ", produced a spindle-shanked, narrow-chested monstrosity that was the mere wraith of the strains that " Parson Jack " and other sportsmen had known and admired and kept pure. The idea, apparently, was to breed a race of terrier to keep pace with hounds, and the supporters of this theory failed to realize the impossibility of producing a Terrier able to accomplish this feat, and at the same time be suited to his real purpose of going to ground. This new production, for all his " lathiness ", was a heavy-weight as compared with the true type, and often scaled as much as 25-lb. The experiment proved a complete failure, for this gimrack " Goliath " among Terriers was unable efficiently to do either of the jobs for which he was designed. But before the reputation of the breed had been irretrievably ruined, wiser

counsels prevailed and a reversion was soon made
·to a sturdier outline. The "Wire" of to-day
shows but slight modifications in the "ideal"
make-up which have taken place since the days of
such model dogs as *Ch. Cackler of Notts* and
Meersbrook Bristles. One of the leaders in the
dethronement of the long-legged upstarts was
Mr. S. E. Shirley, one-time President of the
Kennel Club, who seized with both hands the
opportunity afforded him when judging at an
important show. The Fox Terriers there were a
mixed lot, containing many specimens of the leggy,
lathy, "latest-fashioned" dogs, and a few of the
old-style dogs that could have entered a badger-
earth with more than an even chance of emerging
alive. Mr. Shirley, in making his awards, totally
ignored the new-fangled creations, thus confound-
ing all the late-Victorian advocates of a "slimming
craze" for Fox Terriers. Against such an un-
mistakable gesture by one of the very best judges
of the day their fulminations were of no avail, and
the old-fashioned dog evolved by men who knew
just what a sporting Fox Terrier should be,
resumed his rightful place as the brightest star in

the canine firmament. For the development of the " Wire " as a show-dog during recent years, the fancy is greatly indebted to such far-seeing experts as Mr. A. A. W. Simmonds, Mr. Holland, and Mr. G. Howlett—to say nothing of the efforts of the Wire Fox Terrier Association. The wise guidance of the Association, and the excellent example set by the breeders named and others, are mainly responsible for the uninterrupted progress of the breed since the war, and its immunity from those freakish tendencies which have imperilled, and in some cases definitely blemished, the reputations of certain other breeds. And all lovers and admirers of the " Wire " will hope that he will long continue to be spared the attentions of " friends " with fantastic schemes of improvement, whose real ambition is not to " paint the lily ", but just to " improve the shining hour ".

CHAPTER II

THE "WIRE'S" POPULARITY: SOME REASONS

Figures that cannot lie—Kennel Club registrations—A "one-hundred-per-cent." dog—His courage—His ubiquity—His way with young and old—His tenacity—Honest, handy and hardy—The best "mixer" of all.

EVERY one of the eighty-odd varieties of dog recognized by the English Kennel Club has its faithful band of devotees, varying in number, who have sworn allegiance to their own particular canine fancy. And for every one of these varieties some sound reason, or reasons, could be advanced why large numbers of people have been attracted to them. A short conversation at a show with an exhibitor of almost any breed but the "Wire" breed, and the slightest hint that you are an admirer of his breed, will kindle the light of enthusiasm in the exhibitor's eyes, and if you are sufficiently attuned to his mood, he will tell you that the "Blankhound" or "Dash" Terrier is the only dog in the world worth considering. And if you are wise, and want to see the rest of the show, you will smile an affirmative smile and move on. But the attitude of the exhibitor of the Wired-Haired Fox Terrier is rather different. He knows that there is no necessity for him to justify his preference for the breed, for everybody, even the protagonists of the other breeds, is willing to " hand it " to the great little " Wire ". He is perhaps the one dog in whom the fanciers of all the other breeds can, in their hearts, discern merit. And figures—which in this case cannot lie—show the Wire-Haired Fox Terrier to be the most popular of all breeds. For many years, without interruption, the number of " Wires " registered at the Kennel Club has greatly exceeded the registrations of any other breed—in most years there has been a difference of more than one thousand registrations between the " Wire " and his nearest competitor—who, by the way, is not a Terrier. The " Wire " registrations are nearly three times as many as those of the " runner-up " among the Terriers.

Why is the " Wire " so popular ? In brief, his

admirers are legion because he is a dog one can live with for twenty-four hours a day and fifty-two weeks in a year. Most dogs are courageous, but the " Wire ", bearing in mind his size, is the most conspicuously gallant of dogs. No matter what his owner's sporting proclivities may be, the " Wire " can be fitted into the scheme of things. He is equally the friend and collaborator of the out-of-doors man or woman, and the companion and solace of those who lead the quietest of lives. He, more often than any other, awakens a child's affection for the canine race, and in the evening of many a man's life the friendly muzzle of a " Wire " insinuates itself, understandingly, against its " own god's " knee. " Hold everything " is the " Wire's " motto, he holds on like grim death to his enemies, from the rat to the formidable badger at bay; he holds on just as surely to his friends, although the means of attachment are less tangible. The " secret " of the " Wire's " popularity is no secret: he finds himself on his present pinnacle on merit; no conspiracy of " boosting " could elevate a mediocre dog to such a position, and only an animal possessing, in a superlative degree, all the qualities called for in an all-round utility dog, could attain pre-eminence, and continue to gain in favour, over such a long period. Among the race of dogs he is unsurpassed for ubiquity. He is honest, handy and hardy—and perhaps those three words best sum up his working abilities. The well-to-do and the working-man appreciate equally his sterling worth. Someone has said that if he were marooned on a desert island and had the choice of one living creature as a companion, he would choose a dog. And it is safe to say that more dog-lovers in such a predicament would ask for a " Wire " than for any other breed. He is the best " mixer " of all; a democrat with the bearing of a patrician; a dog who fills the picture wherever he may be. His popularity, to those who know him, gives little cause for wonderment; the wonder is that so many dog-lovers up to now have denied themselves the pleasure and privilege of his companionship.

CHAPTER III

SOME FAMOUS "WIRE" STRAINS: ANCIENT AND MODERN

WITH PARTICULARS OF SOME CHAMPION SIRES AND

DAMS ON THE BENCH

The "Wire" not a recent innovation—XVIth Century
Terriers—XVIIIth Century "Wires"—Bull-terrier and
beagle blood—Early Victorian "Wires"—The "Wires'"
Show *début*—His first Show class—The formation of the
Fox Terrier Club—A "non-sporting" variety!—Jack Russell
Terriers—*Trump, Old Jock, Old Trap,* and *Grove Nettle*—A
"rat-catcher's Terrier"—"Idstone's" unconscious humour—
Major Harding Cox's *Oakleigh Topper*—The Duchess of
Newcastle's *Ch. Cackler of Notts, Coastguard of Notts*
and *Matchmaker*—Some early prices—Lord Lonsdale's
quintet—Major Harding Cox's bad luck—Some famous
dogs of the 'nineties—The founding of the Fox Terrier
Association—Trimming and faking—The Association's
enterprise—The "Wire" during the War—His ever-grow-
ing popularity—Some famous modern breeders' kennels
and dogs—The "Wire" an essentially English breed.

THERE seems to be an impression in some quarters
that the Wire-Haired Fox Terrier is, by compari-
son with his smooth-coated brother, a fairly recent
innovation of obscure ancestry. But it is a fact
which can be well authenticated, that our rugged
friend's history dates back just as far as does that

of the sleek variety. It is generally admitted by students of canine history that both originally derived from the same stock. Terriers of sorts were mentioned and loosely described by various British writers as far back as the sixteenth century, but these appear to have been black-and-tan in colour. With the growth of sport there gradually arose a demand for a dog that could be more easily distinguished from the quarry in the hunting-field, and one of Bewick's engravings executed towards the end of the eighteenth century shows a dog of Fox Terrier type, certainly light in colour and just as certainly rough of coat, that may fairly be accepted as typical of the main race of dogs from which we derive our modern Wire-Haired Terrier. Undoubtedly, admixtures of other blood contributed to his evolution, and it seems to be generally agreed that the Bull Terrier and the Beagle were requisitioned for this purpose. Only of recent years has the " Wire " outvied the smooth in popularity, but as long ago as the 'forties of last century there were " Wires " in plenty in various Midland and other strongholds of the Terrier fancy. Pure-bred Fox Terriers there had un-

doubtedly been for many years ere this, kept by
sportsmen, farmers, gamekeepers, ostlers, and
others who, jealous of the prowess, handsomeness,
and hardiness of their dogs, made every effort,
when breeding, to secure that those qualities
should remain unimpaired in successive generations. Although scientific theories of breeding
had not then been thought of, the instincts of the
men who lived their lives among horses and dogs
in very early Victorian days, guided them aright.
The Wire-Haired Fox Terrier made his show
début in 1860 at Birmingham, but it was not until
1869 that he secured, at Darlington, the distinction
of a show-class all to himself. The important
Birmingham show did not accord him similar
recognition until 1873. The " Wires' " star was
not at that moment in the ascendant, for, until the
formation of the Fox Terrier Club in 1875, he
was subjected to the indignity of being classified in
the Stud Book as a " non-sporting " variety, and
at more than one show of the period the prizes in
the " Wire " classes were withheld on account of
an alleged lack of merit. The fact is, however,
that the judges of those days were sadly at fault,

for some of the dogs so stigmatized became
famous sires, and their influence is seen even
among outstandingly successful strains of to-day.
Even as late as 1879 forces inimical to the well-
being of the " Wires " were still at work, for at
the Kennel Club Show in that year the " Wires "
were removed from the Fox Terrier classification.
One of the very earliest of the adherents of the
Wire-Haired Fox Terrier was the celebrated
Reverend John Russell ("Parson Jack").   He
was breeding Fox Terriers as early as 1815, but
his strain was pre-eminently a working one, and
some of his best dogs in the sporting sense, battle-
scarred and misshapen as they were, would have
stood precious little chance in a show-ring. " Parson " Russell's best-known wired-haired dog was
Trump, which, so the saying goes, he first saw
guarding a milk-cart in Oxford, and bought for a
trifling sum.   *Trump* was the founder of a Wire-
Haired Terrier dynasty that became famous for its
sporting prowess in the West Country.   The most
famous dogs in the early days of showing—dogs
of such renown as *Old Jock* and *Old Trap*—and
the celebrated bitch *Grove Nettle*—were all of the

smooth-coated variety, although *Grove Nettle's* coat was inclined to waviness. Another sporting parson, the Reverend Pearce, whose comments upon various doggy breeds of the day were written under the pseudonym of " Idstone ", was another early champion of the " Wires " in the days when he was contemptuously dubbed a " rat-catcher's Terrier ". " Idstone " was himself the possessor of a "Wire" and made an unconsciously humorous endeavour to popularize the variety among the sportsmen of the day, for the highest recommendation he advanced in its favour was that its thicker coat enabled it to withstand harder thrashings than the " Smooth " ! A staunch adherent of the " Wires " in the days before they may be said to have " arrived " was Major Harding Cox (who, incidentally, was mainly responsible for the formation of the Fox Terrier Club). His famous dog *Oakleigh Topper* proved his quality by winning, at his first show, the Fox Terrier Club's Challenge Cup, beating the best of the then much more fashionable " Smooths ". But the most fortunate day in the history of the " Wires " came when the Duchess of Newcastle decided to transfer her allegiance from Borzois to the heroes of this book. Her Grace laid the foundations of her now famous strain with some magnificent specimens—in fact it is not too much to say that her influence on the breed has been greater than anybody else's. Hers is the strain which, more than any other, has contributed to the make-up of the modern dog. Headed by that great sire, *Champion Cackler of Notts*—how great a dog he was can be judged from a contemporary picture of him by that prince of canine portrait-painters, Arthur Wardle—they have left their mark upon the breed for good. In fact, by a perfectly justifiable process of elimination the descendants of the Duchess of Newcastle's strain hold the field to-day to the exclusion of scions of contemporary " Wire " dynasties of the *Cackler* era, celebrated though some of these were in their day. Some of the Duchess's dogs fetched sensational prices in the days when a pound was worth quite twenty shillings. *Coastguard of Notts* changed hands at £150 when a mere puppy, and others, among them two exceptional dogs in *Coastguard of Notts* and *Matchmaker*, were sold for £250 and £100 respectively. Although Her

SOME FAMOUS "WIRE" STRAINS

Grace was the first breeder of " Wires " whose dogs realized consistently high figures, individual dogs of other strains had been bought and sold for £100 or more some years before the Duchess became interested in the breed. Among the first of these were five dogs purchased on behalf of Lord Lonsdale at the Fox Terrier Club's show at Oxford in 1883, when the quintette, topped by *Briggs* at £200, cost over £600 in all. Unfortunately, this famous sportsman did not reap the reward of this whole-hearted incursion into " Wire " breeding, for although most of his purchases, and *Briggs* especially, had performed prodigies on the bench, they were unable to transmit their undoubted qualities to their offspring. Another celebrated " Wire " of the 'eighties was *Filbert*, otherwise *Pulborough Jumbo*, a dog without a pedigree, who, it was said, had escaped by the purest mischance an early demise in a bucket of water, and had, a little later, a further narrow squeak when his execution had once again been decided upon. He lived to be a prize-winner and sire of distinction, and one of his grandaughters was the famous bitch *Quantock Nettle*, who also was sold for three figures. A little later, Major Harding Cox bought *Cauldwell Nailer* for a hundred guineas, but later repented of his bargain, for he sold the dog back to his former owner for £35. The gallant Major was singularly unfortunate (if we are to accept his own critical standard) with the breeding of " Wires ", for he has confessed in his entertaining reminiscences that he never bred one of sufficiently good quality to compete with the average " V.H.C." dog at a good modern show, although he had owned prominent winners in plenty, and champions too. A great dog in the early 'nineties was Mr. Roper's *Nutcrack*, who later, when in his heyday, was owned by Sir Humphrey de Trafford, and who, during a considerable spell, was well-nigh impregnable upon the show-bench. Sir Humphrey gave £150 for him, and a year or so later sold him for £127. Contemporary with *Nutcrack* was *Tipton Slasher*, belonging to Mr. A. Mutter, who at Birmingham, in a class for Terriers of several breeds, carried off a valuable challenge cup against strong opposition, including Mr. G. Raper's *Go Bang*, who cost his master the then extraordinary sum of £200. A little later these two dogs met formidable opposition in the shape of a dog known as *Money Spinner*, who had previously been shown without much success under the name of *Warwick Royal*. At Derby *Money Spinner* was adjudged the best of the triumvirate, but later, at Manchester, *Go Bang* came out on top, with *Warwick Royal* second. This was probably the true order of merit, and *Go Bang* was subsequently sold to an American fancier for £500. For a number of years prior to the founding of the Wire Fox Terrier Association in 1913 the progress of the Wire-Haired variety remained more or less stationary. Some of the reasons for this stagnation were not far to seek. All sorts of expedients in the preparation of dogs were resorted to by the less scrupulous exhibitors, who took full advantage of the laxity of the rules regarding trimming and faking, and of the diverse interpretations placed upon those rules by different judges. The honest exhibitor who refused to demean himself by such trickery was placed at a grave disadvantage. With the coming of the Association, however, exhibitors for the first time knew exactly what was, and was not, " taboo " in the preparation of their dogs, and the awards began to go to the best dogs instead of to those benched by the most expert fakers.

The Association, also, broke fresh ground in introducing a year-book and register that formed a welcome addition to the periodical literature dealing with the breed. Further, it set itself to amplify the Fox Terrier Club's standard description of the breed, and so well was the work accomplished that it forms an example for the specialist clubs of other breeds. It is given elsewhere in this volume by kind permission of the Wire Fox Terrier Association.

During the war the maintenance of the race of " Wires " had perforce to be left to a large extent to his admirers of the fair sex and, thanks to the valiant efforts, under great difficulties, of the Duchess of Newcastle, Miss Hatfield, and others, the breed was not so hardly hit when peace and dog-shows came once more, as certain other breeds one could name.

Since the year 1919 the cult of the " Wire " has extended to an ever-widening circle, and there are so many first-class breeders with first-class stock, that it would seem the easiest thing in the world for every lover of the breed to own a really good dog. Many owners, however, have still to realize this laudable ambition.

To attempt a comprehensive survey of post-war " Wire " strains and outstanding dogs would be impossible within the scope of a chapter, but the notable names and performances which follow will perhaps give an idea of the status of the " Wire " in Brit'sh dogdom—a status unparalleled in canine history. No attempt is made in the references which follow to place breeders and dogs in any order of merit. But all these ladies and gentlemen have contributed something to the evolution or maintenance of the present standard of a breed that brings more pleasure to dog-lovers than any other.

One of the best known of " Wire " devotees is Mr. A. A. W. Simmonds, whose " Epping " prefix has been in the forefront for many years. The consistent success of his dogs, both on the bench and at stud, over a long period, are evidence of Mr. Simmonds' genius as a breeder and exhibitor. Another name that springs readily to mind is that of Mr. W. Hepwood, of Tilehurst, whose " Dogberry " prefix has greatly distinguished itself at recent shows, and is in much favour with overseas fanciers. *Dogberry Don Juan,* one of the best dogs Mr. Hepwood has produced, is a dual winner of the President's Cup at the Wire Fox Terrier Club's Championship Show. The famous " Crackley " kennels of Mr. J. R. Barlow are known the world over, as might be expected of an establishment that has bred a century of champions during the past decade or so. Mr. Barlow's most celebrated dog (now owned by Mrs. R. C. Bondy) is *Int. Ch. Gallant Fox of Wildoaks,* whose sire and dam were respectively *Int. Ch. Crackley Supreme* and *Int. Ch. Gains Great Surprise.* He is the only International Champion " Wire " in England and has won four Championships in Britain—one on each of the four occasions on which he has been shown. *Gallant Fox's* stud career promises to be as brilliant as his run of show successes. Many of the " Crackley " dogs have crossed the Atlantic to add lustre to American kennels. One of the keenest and cleverest lady breeders is Mrs. E. M. Lester, whose *Ch. Lanarth*

(Upper) BRIG.-GEN., THE LORD ROUNDWAY'S *ROUNDWAY DON JUAN* BY Ch. *CRACKLEY STARTLER* OUT OF *DOGBERRY LOVE BIRD.* A BIG WINNER AND NOTED SIRE.

(Lower) Mrs. R. C. BONDY'S Int. Ch. *GALLANT FOX OF WILDOAKS* BY Int. Ch. *CRACKLEY SUPREME* OUT OF Int. Ch. *GAINS GREAT SURPRISE OF WILDOAKS.*

Bracken, a son of *Ch. Beau Brummel,* has won numerous championship certificates at the principal shows and has, moreover, greatly distinguished himself as a sire. Mrs. Lester has also produced among others, a very excellent dog—both as winner and sire—in *Ch. Lanarth Supreme,* who was sired by the famous *Ch. Crackley Supreme.* A " Wire " breeder whose allegiance dates back over twenty years is Mr. T. Langley Jones, whose bitch *Ch. Talavera Cynthia* has few, if any, equals among her sex. Mr. Jones' dog *Cornwell Caustie* made a most successful *début* at The National Terrier Show, and carried off the Coat Cup at the Great " Wire " Show at Leicester against the strongest possible opposition. Mr. J. Cross's *Grandon Masterpiece* has proved a most brilliant stud dog, and has sired an astonishingly large number of winners. One of the leading Scottish enthusiasts is Mr. J. S. Abbott of Ayr, President of the Scottish Fox Terrier Club. His profound knowledge of the breed is reflected in the splendid dogs which he owns. *Ch. Littleway Nigel* is the best, both as winner and sire, of a fine kennel. A son of Capt. H. R. Phipps's *Ch. Talavera Simon* and *My Luck,* he has himself sired a champion in *Ch. Littleway Brandy Snap,* and a great many other winners at championship shows. Other front rank " Littleway " dogs are *Littleway Peter* and *Littleway Chunky.* The " Weltona " strain, owned by Mr. A. Churchill, have an international reputation. A famous judge of other people's " Wires ", Mr. Churchill's own dogs are of the highest quality. His dog *Weltona Knight* has a long list of winners to his credit, and his bitch *Weltona Shock* is not far removed from perfection. One of the leading lady breeders is Miss L. M. Dixon, the name of whose *Ch. Thet Tetrarch* appears in the pedigrees of so many present-day " Wires " of outstanding quality. *Tetrarch* himself comes of impeccable stock, his sire being the celebrated *Aristocrat* and his dam being the equally famous *Simon's Dimple.* Mention of *Ch. Thet Tetrarch* calls to mind another successful lady breeder in Miss F. J. Esdaile, whose kennel houses some youngsters sired by *Tetrarch* who should ere long create a lasting impression at the leading shows. Miss Esdaile possesses already a first-rate champion in *Ch. Fourwents Rocket.* A compara-

(Upper) Capt. H. R. PHIPPS'S Ch. *TALAVERA SIMON* BY Ch.
FOUNTAIN CRUSADER OUT OF *KINGSTHORPE DONAH.*
SIRE OF 14 CHAMPIONS INCLUDING 9 INTERNATIONAL
CHAMPIONS.
(Lower) Capt. H. R. PHIPPS'S Ch. *TALAVERA JUPITER* BY *BEAU
BRUMMEL OF WILDOAKS* OUT OF *TALAVERA PAULINE.*

tive newcomer to the " Wire " fancy is Brigadier-General Lord Roundway, but the kennel already boasts several excellent specimens, including *Roundway Don Juan* and *Roundway Brunette*, and there is little doubt that with his undoubted eye for both horses and dogs, his Lordship appears likely to attain, very soon, front rank status among " Wire " fanciers. The Talavera kennels, owned by Capt. H. R. Phipps, are invariably mentioned when " Wires " form the topic of conversation, and many well-deserved compliments are paid to *Ch. Talavera Jupiter.*

In the United States of America there is a constant demand for British " Wire " stock. One of the leading kennels is that founded by the late Mr. R. C. Bondy, and now carried on with conspicuous success by Mrs. Bondy. Her *Int. Ch. Gallant Fox of Wildoaks,* although bred in America, comes of a purely British line on both sides, and would shine in any company. *Ch. Weltona Frizette of Wildoaks,* expatriated from England after well-merited triumphs, has repeated her successes against America's best. Mrs. Bondy has many other " stars " in her " Wire " constella-

THE MODERN FOX TERRIER

tion who have demonstrated their worth in the best company on both sides of the Atlantic—among them *Int. Ch. Crackley Supreme*—who is the sire of *Int. Ch. Gallant Fox.* Many other American fanciers are proving remarkably successful in producing first-class " Wires " from home stock, without the aid of recent importations from England, and some of these dogs are well able to hold their own with the best of the immigrants and their offspring.

Enough has been said to show that the Wire-Haired Fox Terrier fancy is rich in the possession of breeders who are for ever striving to maintain and enhance the prestige of a breed that, more than any other, reflects the spirit of the English-speaking nations; an unrivalled combination of gameness, good-temper, and a capacity to stand up unflinchingly against great odds; a staunch friend and bonny fighter. The friends of the breed are ever ready to welcome new admirers of the great little " Wire ", and those who enter the ranks will find everywhere good-fellowship and a general readiness on the part of the " old hands " to place their experience at the disposal of the novice.

(*Upper*) Mrs. R. C. BONDY'S Ch. *BEAU BRUMMEL OF WILDOAKS*
BY Ch. *SIGNAL WARILY OF WILDOAKS* OUT OF Int. Ch.
GAINS GREAT SURPRISE. WINNER OF 8 CHAMPIONSHIPS
AND SIRE OF 8 CHAMPIONS.

(*Lower*) BRIG.-GEN., THE LORD ROUNDWAY'S *ROUNDWAY MAID
OF HONOUR* BY Ch. *TALAVERA JUPITER* OUT OF *FRANVER
QUEENSMAID.*

CHAPTER IV

CHOOSING A " WIRE "

For what purpose ?—Choosing for companionship—The chief
desiderata—The best age to buy a friend—Buying by post
—Dog shops—Prices—The romance of dog-showing—Value
for money—Looking for blemishes—Bitches for companionship—Puppies in transit—Feeding questions—Buying a
show " Wire "—Prices—The field of choice—Breeders not
prophets—The " deposit and approval " system—Puppies
" on appro "—Sporting " Wires "—Buy working strains—
" Jack Russell " Terriers for work—'Ware the faker.

THE first consideration, after a dog-lover has made
the initial decision to acquire a " Wire ", is: For
what purpose is it intended to use the dog ? If
companionship is the main object, the choice is
wide, for although everyone who appreciates a
good dog desires to possess a true-to-type specimen
of his favourite breed, there is no need to exercise
the same meticulous care as in choosing a dog for
a special purpose. Your " Wire " pal who
is just a friend pure and simple will be none the
less affectionate, and your own pleasure will be
just as great if the set or size of his ears would

cause a show-judge to look wistful, or if his stern should not be carried quite at the regulation angle. Neither does it matter if he is a little over-sized. The chief things to look for in a pal-dog are a strong constitution, a good pedigree, an obvious liveliness, and the right sort of coat—hard and wiry, with no suspicion of woolliness. For your real pal, dog or man, is a stout fellow who " legs it " over hill and dale, suitably clad for anything in the weather line. A soft woolly coat would kill the chances of a show specimen, but the same kind of covering on an all-weather pal-dog would probably kill the dog. The best age at which to buy for friendship is at about eight weeks old, for apart from the fact that the very young puppy will then more readily adapt himself to his surroundings, the price will be lower than if the seller has had to keep the puppy in board and lodgings for several weeks longer. Such purchases are best made on the spot, and with such a popular breed there should be no difficulty in making a choice from the stock of a breeder who lives fairly near at hand. Dogs are one of the commodities that should not be bought by post if the purchaser does not wish to run a big risk of making a bad bargain. Dog-shops should, as a rule, be avoided, especially for puppy purchases. The atmosphere of such places with dogs and other animals of all ages drawn together from various sources, is an ideal forcing-ground for all sorts of doggy troubles. The seeker after a puppy should explain his requirements to the breeder. They are, as a rule, honest and understanding people, and when you have indicated what you require, will ask a fair price for likely puppies. It is not possible to lay down hard-and-fast prices for puppies intended as companions, for a good deal depends on the age and strain. Prices for good puppies range from two guineas upwards. And the warning may here be given that if the prospective purchaser of a pal-dog cherishes a secret hope that a puppy purchased for a song may conceivably turn out to be of championship standard, he should straightway dismiss the notion from his mind. The history of dog-showing is full of romances, but this type of romance long ago ceased to happen. Breeders are neither philanthropists nor fools, and are unlikely to under-estimate the potentialities of any of the dogs they offer for sale. However, if this type of bargain is non-existent, the buyer can take certain steps to ensure that he shall have at least good value for his money. The choice should fall upon a healthy puppy, and any other little blemish should not be permitted to over-ride this important point. The chosen puppy's gums and tongue should be of a healthy pink colour. He (or she) should be full of *joie de vivre*, with a rooted objection to being " put upon " by other members of his family, especially when dinner is being served. He should be an obviously good trencherman, and free from any suspicion of rickets, or such annoyances as puppy eczema or other skin trouble. When there is a wide choice of puppies there is no need to purchase a puppy with any of these drawbacks. And, finally, you should *like* the puppy of your choice, even before you've known him for an hour. One says "him" advisedly, for bitches are generally more faithful, sympathetic, and companionable than dogs, and it is well to consider whether these qualities do not compensate for those awkward spells of two or three weeks that occur twice a year when vigilance is necessary.

CHOOSING A "WIRE"

Having taken possession of your purchase, care should be taken to guard against exposure on the way home. Cars and trains are upsetting to little dogs unaccustomed to travelling, and it is well to go prepared with a basket or well-ventilated box lined at the bottom with some soft absorbent material. On reaching home the "new chum" should be given a saucer of warm milk and made comfortable in some warm, draughtproof corner on a bed in a box or basket raised from the floor-level. The new owner should ascertain from the seller what food the puppy has been accustomed to having, and should adhere strictly to that dietary for the first few days. The pal-puppy's progress, both as regards feeding and training, is dealt with in a later chapter.

Buying a "Wire" with the fixed intention of showing him is rather a different proposition. The first question to be decided is that of price. There is almost as wide a range of prices for "Wires" of show standard as there is for houses or diamond rings. But one golden rule should, from the buyer's point of view, govern every purchase of a puppy intended for show, and that is, buy the best you can afford. Prices for puppies of recognized show strains, who themselves are regarded as being potential show-dogs, range from five or six guineas upwards. This decision reached, the field of choice narrows, and if you are a novice it is best to rely upon the advice of someone who has a good knowledge of the breed. If none such are to be found among your acquaintance it is best to go to a well-accredited breeder, lay your cards on the table and trust to his integrity to " deliver the goods ". Breeders are not soothsayers, and their forecasts of the future are not always realized. But if you ask for the best puppy of a litter and are prepared to pay the price asked, you may rely upon getting what the breeder honestly considers the best of the bunch. Do not, under any circumstances, purchase a puppy of alleged show class without first seeing it. This method of purchase may be all very well when seeking a dog of more mature age, when the " deposit and approval " system run by the dog newspapers can operate. No sane breeder will send a very young puppy " on appro ". He may catch all kinds of diseases on the way, and be either a great trial to the purchaser or a danger to the rest of the breeder's stock if returned. As already mentioned, the prices of puppies of show quality vary greatly, and one would be lucky indeed if one's purchase of a puppy with a modest pedigree were to culminate in the winning of a red ticket at Cruft's or the Kennel Club Show. Such things do happen, but the only way to ensure a sporting chance of gaining such a distinction is to buy the best puppy available—and, naturally, he will cost a good deal.

When a puppy is required for sporting purposes the foregoing considerations do not weigh so much in the quest for the right dog—although some of the sporting strains are equally at home upon the bench, and are not lacking in those qualities that appeal to show judges. The modern Fox Terrier breeders have not made the mistake of producing a dog for show purposes that is an entirely different creature from the dog that proves his worth to sportsmen up and down the countryside. Certain sporting breeds have had to face the accusation that their show specimens are a race apart from the working members of the breed, but the " Wires " who really adorn the show-bench would undoubtedly enter with zest into the job of bolting a fox, or a " spot " of badger-digging. But is would be a waste of good money to pay a high price for a puppy from some aristocratic show strain with the idea of using it merely for sporting purposes. The more sensible plan would be to obtain a puppy bred from generations of genuine working " Wires ". Such are to be found in all parts of the country where field sports are indulged in. They are to be found in kennels of hounds, among the farming and game-keeping fraternities, and also among those gentle-men of the countryside whose movements are somewhat mysterious. There are still to be found, too, the sporting variety known as " Jack Russell " Terriers. There is not the same advantage in buying a very young puppy for purely sporting purposes, but it is just as advisable to see the dog before you buy. Otherwise, if the transaction is being conducted by post, the " deposit and approval " system conducted by the dog-papers should be insisted on—as there are some real artists at the game of faking dogs (and also advertisements) whose special line is selling so-called sporting " Wires ". After all, the sporting Terrier is called upon to perform stiffer tasks than his brother of the show-ring and the domestic hearth. He must be a dog of high mettle, intelligence, strength, and stamina. The nondescript animals that are so often foisted upon unsuspecting buyers are likely to prove absolutely useless for sport; the combination of qualities so imperative in a sporting dog are the result of careful selective breeding of long lines of working Terriers on both sides. And the sportsman should make just as certain of getting a real " honest-to-goodness " " Wire " as the man with show ambitions.

CHAPTER V

TRAINING THE "WIRE"

The introduction of the puppy—His night quarters—First
steps in house-training—Corporal punishment—A revolt-
ing practice—Mutual self-respect—Points of etiquette—
Puppy playthings—Verbal commands—Outdoor behaviour
—Collar or harness ?—Leads—Keeping to heel—Sleep—
Receiving callers—Garden manners—Introduction to sport
—Hasten slowly—The hunting instinct—Fox and badger
earth—Going to ground—Badger-digging—Otter hunting—
The "Wire" as gun dog—Rabbits—Fox Terriers in
France—The show puppy's routine.

(a) THE DOMESTIC DOG   (b) THE SHOW DOG

(c) THE SPORTING DOG

THE training of a "Wire" puppy destined to
become a friend of the family proceeds, during
the first few months of his training, on the same
lines as his brother whose ultimate destination is
the bench. In fact, most one-dog owners treat
their show dog, even though he be a champion,
just the same in the domestic circle as if he were
the ordinary tramp-scarer, companion-hiker and
fireside *vis-à-vis*.

TRAINING THE "WIRE"

Let us begin with the arrival of the new puppy at your home. He will probably be very tired, if he has travelled an appreciable distance, and after the first introductions have been made and the family have all agreed what a perfect dear he is, he will want to sleep. When he awakens in the night he will probably experience a feeling of utter desolation, and will interrupt the peaceful slumbers of the household with his protests. It is best to give the puppy a bed in the corner of one's bedroom for the first few nights. A few soothing words from a human being close at hand will usually allay his feelings in the small hours, whereas, if he is kept in the kitchen, the bellowed admonitions from the upper regions are liable to make him all the more disturbed.

The first step in the training of the domestic dog is to make him clean in the house. This is one of the things that no puppy learns by instinct, but some are much quicker than others to realize what is required. The best plan after each transgression is to put the puppy outside immediately, with a mild shaking and audible expressions of disgust. There is absolutely no need to administer

47

corporal punishment to puppies of tender age. They are extremely sensitive to the spoken word and a shaking. And they should be given every opportunity to be clean by being placed outside many times a day, without waiting for an offence to take place. A useful plan recommended, especially to flat-dwellers, is to train the young dog first to use a tray of ashes, or even an old newspaper placed on the floor. After a little while the puppy realizes what is required, and when, after a few days, the tray or paper is placed out of doors, cleanly habits are already being formed. On no account should the revolting practice be indulged in of soiling a puppy in order to teach him to be clean. He hates it, and it is one of the things that contribute to the spoiling of a puppy's spirit. Throughout the training of a dog kindly methods should prevail. The normally treated dog is most anxious to please his master, not because of the fear of punishment, but because he knows that he will receive his due meed of praise. Dog-ownership should be a partnership based on mutual self-respect, and in the writer's experience the mailed-fist

policy merely produces a cringing servility.
Concurrently with the foregoing aspect of the
training there are other points of etiquette to be
taught. Cushions and upholstery, divans and
eiderdowns are very inviting, but the puppy must
be taught to resist these temptations—and if his
box or basket contains a soft piece of old blanket
there is every inducement to resist the temptation
offered by other soft spots in the house. The
average healthy puppy's lust for destruction must
be diverted into inexpensive channels; an old
slipper of substantial make; a dog ball (one that
is too big for him to swallow) and a large sized
bone, perfectly dry and clean, are toys to be
recommended as likely to save their worth a
thousandfold in curtains, carpets, and chair-legs
that the puppy will otherwise inevitably attack.
All forms of disobedience should be immediately
reproved with a stern " No ", and in the earliest
stages of puppyhood it is important that this word
should be understood and acted upon as soon as
possible. All tendency to jump up at, or upon,
visitors should be discouraged, as most people,
even close friends, object to a sprinkling of white

49

D

hairs on their clothing as souvenirs of their visit. The puppy's outdoor behaviour also calls for a series of lessons. The first, and most important, is in keeping to heel. Many puppies object most strongly to wearing a collar or harness. This matter should be taken in hand very early, and the puppy should be accustomed to wearing the insignia of civilization indoors for increasingly long periods each day. For the young puppy, harness is preferable to a collar as the strain on a lead is distributed over a wider area, and is consequently less liable to cause injury. When the puppy has become used to harness or collar he can be taken out on a lead, into some quiet street. The lead should be long and light—a piece of strong cord is best. The puppy's inclination to go in the opposite direction to your own should be discouraged by gentle pulls on the cord—care being taken to avoid violent jerks and tugging. At the same time the command " Heel " should be given, and this word should be rigidly adhered to throughout his training when he is required to come to heel. This stage of the training should be carefully graduated, and the young puppy should not be exercised to the point of exhaustion.

TRAINING THE "WIRE"

At first, a few minutes each day is sufficient. The training, or at any rate the groundwork, should be undertaken only by the dog's rightful master. If other members of the family are allowed to take a hand, the result of the multiplicity of commands meaning the same thing is that an utter confusion arises in the little dog's logical mind. The average well-trained dog understands an extraordinarily large number of words, but the use of synonyms places an unfair tax upon his intelligence. After a while the puppy can be allowed off the lead where distractions are absent, and encouraged to keep to heel. Any tendency to drag behind or to run on ahead should be repressed with a light tap of the hand and the command "Heel" uttered at the same time. The very young puppy should be allowed plenty of sleep, especially after exercise, and he should be protected from any well-meaning attentions from children and others that would interfere with his "forty winks" when he feels so disposed. He must be taught to recognize the footsteps of the regular callers at the house—personal friends, tradesmen, postmen, and others—and to reserve his barking to draw attention to the unaccustomed visitor. A dog can be trained in garden manners too. There is no reason why he should be allowed to soil choice shrubs with impunity, or bury unwanted bones in the borders. House-training the average dog is mainly a matter of patience, and he can be almost as easily taught that certain places out of doors are sacrosanct. When you are looking forward to " giving your heart to a dog to tear " for ten or twelve years it is worth while going to some pains for a few months to ensure that he shall be a model of doggy decorum. It is not enough that he should, as Dr. John Caius puts it so picturesquely, defend his master " from the invasion of villons and theefes, preserving their lyfes from losse, and their health from hassard, theyr fleshe from hacking and hewing with such like desperate daungers ". In the long and tranquil spells between such emergencies he should be a lover of law and order, and a little gentleman, and if he is lacking in social qualities it is nearly always his master's own fault.

The training of a " Wire " intended for sport or the show bench progresses during the first few months along the same lines as those of his purely domestic brother, for until the normal puppy is at least six months' old he has not the strength to stand up to his natural enemies. It is never wise to over-rate the capacity of a puppy to deal with rats and even bigger creatures, and his first introduction to sport should be in the nature of an object-lesson given by mature dogs while the puppy, on a leash, or otherwise under firm control, plays the part of onlooker. To awaken his latent instincts he may be allowed to make contact with a defunct fox, but if he is permitted to indulge in conflict with an animal at bay before his physical equipment is equal to the task, he may sustain severe damage, and ever after show a distaste for the work. It is a common practice among those who train Terriers, to bring them into contact with the skins of the animals they will be required to hunt. The development of the hunting instinct is a natural process, and the most that can be done by the owner is to let the dog watch experienced, older dogs at work and get him accustomed to the sights and smells associated with the sport in which the pupil will specialize. A young dog should never be forced into a fox or badger earth; when he feels the urge himself to go to ground he will need no compulsion. His instinct, plus the spirit of emulation upon seeing what the older dogs are doing, will bring rapid progress in the course of a few days. At six months or so the normal puppy may be introduced to a rat, but this step should never be taken if it is felt that the rodent is likely to give the youngster a punishing time. His introduction to Master Brock should be nicely graduated. As a rule, when young dogs are present at a badger-dig they are only allowed to have a " go ", if at all, when the diggers have come close to the badger and the passage has been enlarged. Then they are permitted to show their mettle for a little while before one of the diggers hauls out the badger by his tail. The best " Wires " for badger-digging are the " Jack Russell " variety, although any specimen of quality would be likely to put up a good show. In general " make-up " a good working Fox Terrier should, apart from the head, look like a " pocket edition " of a first-class Foxhound.

For otter-hunting, Terriers of longer-legged

breeds are usually preferred as being more useful than the " Wire ", but the latter finds his place in many otter hunts, being called upon to execute many an " ejectment order " when the otter is obstinately inclined to remain in her holt.

A good many " Wires " have been converted into quite creditable gun-dogs, retrieving game as efficiently as a first-class dog of one of the *pukka* gun-dog breeds. For the owner fired with an ambition to train a " Wire " as a gun-dog, a study of one of the books specially devoted to the subject is recommended. But the dog who has had a spell of rabbit-hunting is unlikely to develop sufficient concentration on higher quarry to make him of any practical use in territory where " bunny " abounds as an irresistible counter-attraction.

It is a great compliment to the breed that the French, who have a great many more opportunities for badger-digging than ourselves, prefer a Fox Terrier above all other dogs for bolting the fox or entering the badger's earth. The French dog is of a uniform size, and the same small type is used to meet both fox and badger underground.

THE MODERN FOX TERRIER

The "Wire" in puppyhood, as already said, leads much the same sort of existence whatever his destiny, and the best foundation on which to build a dog's show reputation is a natural, healthy existence with good and suitable food; ample and regular daily exercise; hygienic sleeping and living conditions; and thorough daily grooming. The special, intensive grooming, conditioning and training in ring deportment that should precede a show come later and are dealt with in the chapter regarding preparation for show.

CHAPTER VI

THE WIRE-HAIRED FOX TERRIER

STANDARD DESCRIPTION AND SCALE OF POINTS

THE writer is indebted to Mr. A. A. W. Simmonds, the indefatigable Honorary Secretary of the Wire Fox Terrier Association, for his kind permission to reproduce here the Association's standard description of the breed: —

(i) DESCRIPTION OF THE WIRE FOX TERRIER

The following is the description of Points of the Wire Fox Terrier as adopted by the Association at a General Meeting held on February 12th, 1913, at Cruft's Show, London.   This description is mainly an amplification of the standard as laid down by the Fox Terrier Club, and the terms which are identical with the standard are printed in italics.   It is considered that this description, which has been drawn up, revised, and approved

THE MODERN FOX TERRIER

by many of the leading owners of " Wires " of
the present day, will be of material assistance to
the smaller owners and to the novice breeder.

Nose.—*Should be black.*

Foreface.—Although the foreface *should
gradually taper* from eye to muzzle and should
dip slightly at its juncture with the forehead, it
should not " dish " or *fall away* quickly below the
eyes, where it should be full and well made up,
but relieved from " wedginess " by a little delicate
chiselling. Both upper and lower jaws *should be
strong* and *muscular*, the *teeth as nearly as possible
level* and capable of closing together like a vice—
the lower canines locking in front of the upper—
and the points of the upper incisors slightly over-
lapping the lower. While well-developed jaw-
bones, armed with a set of strong, white teeth,
impart that appearance of strength to the foreface
which is so desirable in the Wire-Haired variety,
an excessive bony or muscular development of the
jaw is both unnecessary and unsightly, as it is
partly responsible for the full and rounded con-
tour of the cheeks to which the term " cheeky "
is applied.

58

EYES.—*Should be dark in colour*, moderately *small* and not prominent, *full of fire, life and intelligence; as nearly as possible circular in shape*, and not too far apart. Anything approaching a yellow eye is most objectionable.

SKULL.—The top line of the *skull* should be *almost flat, sloping* slightly and gradually *decreasing in width towards the eyes*, and should not exceed $3\frac{1}{2}$ inches in diameter at the widest part—measuring with the calipers—in the full grown dog of correct size, the bitch's skull being proportionately narrower. If this measurement is exceeded the skull is termed " coarse ", while a full grown dog with a much narrower skull is termed " bitchy " in the head. The length of the head of a full-grown well-developed dog of correct size—measured with the calipers from the back of the occipital bone to the nostrils—should be from 7 to $7\frac{1}{4}$ inches, the bitch's head being proportionately shorter. Any measurement in excess of this usually indicates an over-sized or long-backed specimen, although occasionally—so rarely as to partake of the nature of a freak—a Terrier of correct size may boast a head $7\frac{1}{2}$ inches in length. In a well-balanced head there should be little apparent difference in length between skull and foreface. If, however, the foreface is noticeably shorter, it amounts to a fault, the head looking weak and " unfinished ". On the other hand, when the eyes are set too high up in the skull, and too near the ears, it also amounts to a fault, the head being said to have a " foreign appearance ".

EARS.—*Should be small and V-shaped and of moderate thickness,* the flaps neatly folded over *and dropping forward close to the cheeks.* The top line of the folded ear should be well above the level of the skull. A pendulous ear, hanging dead by the side of the head like a hound's is uncharacteristic of the Terrier, while an ear which is semi-erect is still more undesirable.

NECK.—*Should be clean, muscular, of fair length, free from throatiness,* and presenting a graceful curve when viewed from the side.

SHOULDERS.—When viewed from the front should slope, steeply downwards from their juncture with the neck towards *the points,* which *should be fine.* When viewed from the side they *should be long, well laid back,* and should slope obliquely backward from points to *withers, which should always be clean cut.* A shoulder well laid back gives the long fore-hand which, in combination with a short back, is so desirable in Terrier or Hunter.

CHEST.—*Deep and not broad,* a too narrow chest being almost as undesirable as a very broad one. Excessive depth of chest and brisket is an impediment to a Terrier when going to ground.

BODY.—The back should be *short* and level, *with no appearance of slackness—the loins* muscular and *very slightly arched.* The brisket should be deep, *the front ribs moderately arched,* and *the back ribs deep,* and well sprung. The term "slackness" is applied both to the portion of the back immediately behind the withers when it shows any tendency to dip, and also the flanks, when there is too much space between the back-ribs and hip-bone. When there is little space between the ribs and hips, the dog is said to be "short in couplings", "short-coupled" or "well-ribbed-up". A Terrier can scarcely be too short in back, provided he has sufficient length of neck and liberty of movement. The bitch may be slightly longer in couplings than the dog.

HIND-QUARTERS.—*Should be strong and muscular, quite free* from droop or crouch; the *thighs long and powerful;* the stifles well curved and turned neither in nor out; the *hock-joints* well bent and *near the ground;* the hocks perfectly upright and parallel with each other when viewed from behind. The worst possible form of hind-quarters consists of a short second-thigh and a straight stifle, a combination which causes the hind-legs to act as props rather than as instruments of propulsion.

STERN.—*Should be set on rather high and carried gaily, but not curled. It should be of good strength* and substance and of fair length—a three-quarters dock is about right—since it affords the only safe grip when handling working Terriers. A very short tail is suitable neither for work nor show.

LEGS.—*Viewed from any direction should be straight,* the bone *of the fore-legs strong* right down to the feet. *The elbows should hang perpendicular to the body, working free of the sides, both fore- and hind-legs being carried straight through in travelling.*

.FEET.—*Should be round, compact, and not large*—the pads *tough* and well-cushioned, and *the toes moderately arched and turned neither in nor out.* A Terrier with good-shaped fore-legs and feet will wear his nails down short by contact with the road surface, the weight of the body being evenly distributed between the toe-pads and the heels. Out-turned feet, heavy ears, and indifferent hocks are three of the commonest faults of the present-day " Wire ".

COAT.—The principal difference between that of the Smooth and Wire variety is that, whereas the former is *straight and flat,* that of the latter appears to be *broken*—the hairs having a tendency to twist. The best coats are of a *dense, wiry* texture—like cocoa-nut matting—the hairs growing so closely and strongly together that when parted with the fingers the skin cannot be seen. At the base of these stiff hairs is a shorter growth of finer and softer hair—termed the under-coat. The coat on the sides is never quite so hard as that on the back and quarters. Some of the hardest coats are " crinkly " or slightly waved, but a curly coat is very objectionable. The hair on the upper and lower jaws should be crisp and only sufficiently long to impart an appearance of strength to the fore-face, thus effectually differentiating them from the Smooth variety. The hair on the fore-legs should be also dense and crisp. The coat should average in length from ¾ to 1 inch on shoulders and neck, lengthening to 1½ inches on withers, backs, ribs, and quarters. These measurements are given rather as a guide to exhibitors than as an infallible rule, since the length of coat varies in different specimens and seasons. The judge must form his own opinion as to what constitutes a " sufficient " coat.

COLOUR.—*White should predominate; brindle, red, liver,* or slatey blue *are objectionable. Otherwise, colour is of little or no importance.*

CHARACTER.—The Terrier should be alert, quick of movement, keen of expression, on the tip-toe of expectation at the slightest provocation. Character is imparted by the expression of the eyes and by the carriage of ears and tail.

SIZE.—*Bone and strength in a small compass*

are essential, but this must not be taken to mean a Terrier should be " cloddy ", or in any way coarse—speed and endurance being requisite as well as power. The Terrier must on no account be leggy, nor must he be too short on the leg. He should stand like a cleverly-made short-backed hunter, covering a lot of ground. According to present-day requirements, a full-sized, well-balanced dog should not exceed $15\frac{1}{2}$ inches at the withers—the bitch being proportionately lower—nor should the length of back from wither to root of tail exceed 12 inches, while, to maintain the relative proportions, the head—as before mentioned—should not exceed $7\frac{1}{4}$ inches or be less than 7 inches. A dog with these measurements should scale 18 lbs. in show condition—a bitch weighing some 2 lbs. less—with a margin of 1 lb. either way.

BALANCE.—This may be defined as the correct proportions of a certain point or points, when considered in relation to a certain other point, or points. It is the key-stone of the Terrier's anatomy. The chief points for consideration are the relative proportions of skull and fore-face;

head and back; height at withers and length of body from shoulder-point to buttock—the ideal of proportion being reached when the last two measurements are the same. It should be added that, although the head measurements can be taken with absolute accuracy, the height at withers and length of back and coat are approximate, and are inserted for the information of breeders and exhibitors rather than as a hard-and-fast rule.

MOVEMENT.—Movement, or action, is the crucial test of conformation. The Terrier's legs should be carried straight forward while travelling, the fore-legs hanging perpendicular and swinging parallel with the sides, like a pendulum of a clock. The principal propulsive power is furnished by the hind legs, perfection of action being found in the Terrier possessing long thighs and muscular second thighs well bent at the stifles, which admit of a strong forward thrust or "snatch" of the hocks. When approaching, the fore-legs should form a continuation of the straight of the front, the feet being the same distance apart as the elbows. When stationary, it is often difficult to determine whether a dog is slightly out at

THE WIRE-HAIRED FOX TERRIER

shoulder, but, directly he moves, the defect—if it exists—becomes more apparent, the fore-feet having a tendency to cross, " weave " or " dish ". When, on the contrary, the dog is tied at the shoulder, the tendency of the feet is to move wider apart, with a sort of paddling action. When the hocks are turned in—cow-hock—the stifles and feet are turned outwards, resulting in a serious loss of propulsive power. When the hocks are turned outwards the tendency of the hind feet is to cross, resulting in an ungainly waddle.

N.B.—Old scars or injuries, the result of work or accident, should not be allowed to prejudice a Terrier's chance in the show-ring, unless they interfere with its movements or with its utility for work or stud.

(ii) THE SCALE OF VALUES OF INDIVIDUAL POINTS

(As recommended by the Fox Terrier Club)

1. Head and Ears 15
2. Neck 5
3. Shoulders and Chest 10
4. Back and Loin 10
5. Hind Quarters 15

THE MODERN FOX TERRIER

6. Stern 5
7. Legs and Feet 15
8. Coat 15
9. Symmetry, Size, and Character 10

——

Total ... 100

——

DISQUALIFYING POINTS

1. NOSE.—White, cherry, or spotted to a considerable extent with either these colours.
2. EARS.—Prick, tulip, or rose.
3. MOUTH.—Much undershot or much overshot.

THE POINTS OF A TERRIER

(as illustration, page 69)

1. The Forehead.
2. Junction of Forehead and Nose.
3. The Nose (muzzle).
4. Nostrils.
5. Muzzle (proper).
6. The Temple.
7. The Ears.
8. The Occiput.

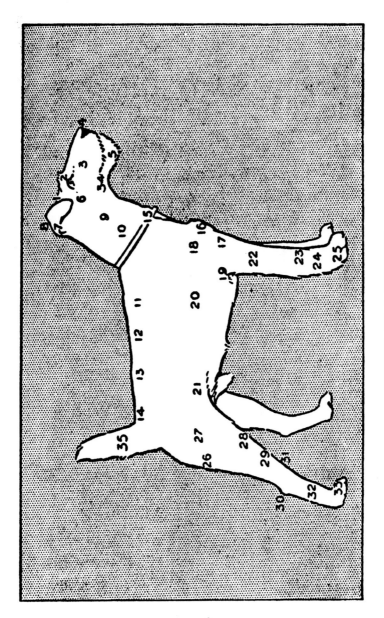

POINTS OF A TERRIER

69

9. Posterior Angle of Jaw.
10. The Neck.
11. The Withers.
12. The Saddle.
13. The Loins.
14. Croup.
15. Dewlap.
16. Brisket.
17. The Arm.
18. The Shoulder.
19. Point of Elbow.
20. Ribs and Chest Wall.
21. Flank.
22. Forearm.
23. Knee or Waist.
24. Pastern.
25. Toes.
26. Buttock.
27. First Thigh.
28. Stifle.
29. Second Thigh.
30. Point of Hock.
31. Front Face of Hock.
32. Pastern.

33. Toes.
34. Cheeks.
35. Stern.

(iii) SPECIALIST CLUBS

(a) *Great Britain and Ireland*

Barnsley Fox Terrier Club.
Birmingham Fox Terrier Club.
Bolton Fox Terrier Club.
Bristol Fox Terrier Club.
Chester Fox Terrier Club.
Chesterfield Fox Terrier Club.
Cumberland Fox Terrier Club.
Derby Fox Terrier Club.
Fox Terrier Association of Ireland.
Fox Terrier Club.
Irish Fox Terrier Club.
London Airedale and Fox Terrier Club.
Manchester Fox Terrier Club.
Mansfield Woodhouse Fox Terrier Club.
North Staffordshire Fox Terrier Association.
Northumberland & Durham Fox Terrier Club.
Notts Fox Terrier Club.
Oldham Fox Terrier Club.

THE MODERN FOX TERRIER

Rhondda Airedale and Fox Terrier Club.
Rochdale Fox Terrier Club.
Scottish Fox Terrier Club.
Sheffield Wire Fox Terrier Club.
Sunderland Fox Terrier Club.
Ulster Fox Terrier Club.
West of England Fox Terrier Club.
Western Fox Terrier Breeders' Association.
Wire Fox Terrier Association.
Wire Fox Terrier Association of Ireland.
Working Pedigree Fox Terrier Association.
Yorkshire Wire-Hair Fox Terrier Association.

(b) *Overseas*

Alberta Fox Terrier Association.
American Fox Terrier Club.
British Columbia Fox Terrier Association.
Fox Terrier Association of New South Wales.
Fox Terrier Verband.
Reunion des Amateurs de Fox Terriers.
Victoria Airedale and Fox Terrier Association.

CHAPTER VII

PREPARATION FOR SHOW AND SHOWING

Age to begin—Registration—Show successes—The different
kinds of show—The various show classes—The puppy's
show *début*—Joining a specialist Club—The Kennel Club's
regulations for show preparation—Discreditable conduct—
Recent regulations and their effect—Risks the fakers run—
The professional trimmer—What trimming is—Grooming
—Coat condition important — Washing — Woolliness —
Brushes and hand-gloves—Exercise—Dangers of damp—
Care of the feet—Show rehearsals—Handling, bad and
good—Professional handlers—The day of the Show—
Handling is an art—Some unwritten laws of showing—
The dog's show needs—Learning to lose.

THE serious preparation of a puppy for show will
not begin until he is nearing six months old, for
except at Sanction Shows puppies under that age
cannot be shown.   Even at six months most
sensible owners agree that shows are not good for
a puppy's health—apart from the fact that he has
to compete with older and therefore more fully-
developed dogs.

The first essential to showing at any show
worthy the name is registration of the puppy at

the Kennel Club, and this can be done concurrently with the entry of the puppy for his first show. In the papers devoted to canine matters, lists of forthcoming shows appear with the names and addresses of the Secretaries, to whom application should be made for a schedule. When received it will be accompanied by the necessary form of application for registration, which should be completed and forwarded to the Kennel Club with the regulation fee of half-a-crown. This fee is doubled if either or both parents are unregistered. A Sanction Show is the minor sort of affair for which Kennel Club sanction has been obtained. The arrangements are as a rule informal, without any pretence at benching or the other paraphernalia of the more important types of dog-show. Members' Shows are a step higher, and are properly organized shows with rings and benches, but confined exclusively to the members of the specialist clubs, under whose auspices they are held. At an Open Show, wherever held, the exhibits are drawn from a wide area and as a consequence the opposition is likely to be formidable. The difference between an Open Show and a Championship Show is that at the former challenge certificates are not awarded. If your puppy has any pretensions to real class it is best to avoid the Sanction and Members' Shows, and enter for a suitable class or classes in an Open Show. In an Open Show there are Puppy and Junior Classes, for dogs from six to twelve months' old, and from six to eighteen months' old respectively, and there is obviously likely to be greater obstacles to a young puppy's success in the Novice Class. There are also Maiden, Débutant, and Novice Classes, where the opposition will probably be even more formidable. As to what classes are best for your puppy's show *début*, in this matter it is best to rely upon the advice of seasoned exhibitors, and if you have joined a specialist club —as you should if you propose to treat your showing seriously—you will not lack honest and wise counsel from your fellow members, given freely and cheerfully for the asking. Having settled this point—and it is an important one which may make or mar your puppy's career— next comes the job of getting him into show trim and of getting yourself into show trim as well if you aspire to be the handler. But let us take the dog first—and here it may be opportune to refer to the regulations laid down by the Kennel Club as to the preparation of dogs for exhibition. Formerly, these regulations contained a formidable array of prohibited and permitted practices, and substances that might or might not be utilized in preparing dogs for exhibition. But on the 11th October, 1932, the Kennel Club redrafted and considerably shortened the regulations on this matter. The regulations as they now stand are commendably brief, and stipulate that: —

" A dog shall be disqualified from winning any award at any Show (except as hereinafter provided), and the person or persons responsible for its exhibition may be dealt with under Kennel Club Rule 17, if it be proved to the Committee of the Show or the Committee of the Kennel Club, as the case may be: —

1. That any dye, colouring, darkening, bleaching, or other matter has been used for the purpose of improving the colour, marking, or texture of the coat of a dog.

2. That if any cutting, piercing, breaking by

force, or any kind of operation or act which alters the anatomical formation, or colour, of the dog, or any part thereof, has been practised, or anything done calculated, in the opinion of the Committee of the Kennel Club, to deceive, except in cases of necessary operation which must be certified by a qualified veterinary surgeon. Dewclaws may be removed in any breed, and shortening the tails of dogs of the following breeds will not render them *liable to disqualification* "

Then follows a list of breeds which includes the Fox Terrier. The Rule 17 mentioned lays down the penalties for discreditable conduct.

Some of the best-known people in the world of " Wires " have expressed grave apprehension as to the effect of the deletion from these regulations of specifically prohibited practices. They maintain that the regulations as they now stand will react to the detriment of the breed; but these fears are almost certainly unfounded. Regulations notwithstanding, the faker is with us always, and his wiles can quite easily be countered by judges who apply an intelligent interpretation of the regulations as now revised. It is clear that to use foreign substances for improving the coat or do anything calculated to deceive, renders the faker liable to be penalized for discreditable conduct.

Preparation of a dog for show consists of an intensive course of exercising, grooming, conditioning, and accustoming the dog to comport himself well in the show-ring. The trimming of a " Wire ", until the owner has acquired the art, is best left in the hands of a professional trimmer who knows exactly how to make the most of a dog's coat. Mainly this operation consists in removing the dead hair in a manner that puts the coat in the best possible shape. The actual condition of the coat itself is, of course, a matter for the owner, and a thorough daily grooming with dandy brush, and regular cleaning with hot bran, well rubbed into the coat and brushed out, will help to bring it into first-class condition. It should be remembered that coat condition is one of the chief points of a " Wire ". Washing the coat should be avoided unless absolutely necessary, as it makes for woolliness, when it is desirable that the texture should be as hard and wiry as possible.

PREPARATION FOR SHOW

A dandy brush (there are qualities specially made for " Wires ") and comb (not a steel-toothed one as it is liable to break the coat) and a hand-glove for putting on the final touches are all the toilet requisites usually needed. And if it should be imperative to wash the dog, as, for instance, after he has rolled in some evil-smelling substance—care should be taken to avoid soaps of an alkaline nature or those containing carbolic.

As for exercise, when the puppies have reached the age of three months they may be given as much exercise in the open air as they are able to take, so long as they have a draught-proof and dry place to rest in when they feel so inclined. Damp should at all costs be avoided, and a concrete run is preferable to grass, not only because it dries quickly, but helps to harden the feet. Where a concrete or paved run is not available the puppies should have daily exercise on a hard road, as well as a run in some field at every favourable opportunity, but the feet should be always examined on reaching home, and any traces of grit or tar removed. The latter can be dissolved by using a little fresh butter as a solvent. There is no need to refrain from giving puppies their daily run in wet weather so long as they are given a thorough rub-down immediately upon their return. One of the most important things in training for show is to accustom the dog as far as possible to the sights, sounds, and general atmosphere of a show-ring, and to the presence of crowds of people. The latter is easily rehearsed by taking the dog into crowded thoroughfares, but the reproduction of the show atmosphere calls for rather more effort. It is worth going to this trouble, for many a dog has had his chances of a prize irretrievably ruined in the show ring through being overwhelmed by the strangeness of his surroundings, and consequently unable to do himself justice. An excellent imitation of a ring can be made by assembling all available chairs in a good-sized room, or even in the garden, and then mustering all available members of the household, who should be encouraged to keep up an incessant running fire of chatter and laughing, rustling of papers, dropping of handbags and other articles from laps—endeavouring to do most of the things that people sitting around a show-ring invariably do. The rest of the usual ordeal should be reproduced, too, if possible—the presence of other dogs on leads in close proximity, and the judge's examination. This last may prove rather difficult, as the rôle should preferably be undertaken by someone whom the dog doesn't know well—and there may be decided objections on the part of the " actor " cast for the part when all the little bits of " business " are explained to him—examination of teeth, limbs and generally overhauling a strange dog. However, it is worth while making a serious effort to obviate any danger of show-shyness, for there can be nothing more disappointing that to bench a dog in top-notch condition and then be robbed of one's just reward through stage-fright.

An even more important matter is the handling of the dog in the ring. A good deal depends upon the manner in which the dog is presented to the eye of the judge. The standard description of the " Wire " says that he should be " alert, quick of movement, keen of expression, and on the tip-toe of expectation ". The dog who is badly handled is hardly likely to display these qualities to the full. The accomplished handler is able to get the best out of a dog, and it is almost impossible for a novice, unless he be a genius, to handle a " Wire " with any hope of success in the ring. The really competent handlers, many of whom gain their livelihood in the show-ring, have only acquired the art after years of experience, and the novice who aspires to handle his own dogs should take every opportunity of watching the handlers of the leading dogs at work and of getting them to talk—for like most " Wire " enthusiasts in other directions, they make no secret of their methods; it is the " touch " of the expert that means so much.

As the day of the show approaches the grooming should be carried out with the utmost thoroughness, and everything possible should be done to ensure that the dog shall arrive at the show in the pink of condition, for a dog out of sorts is obviously unable to give of his best. The hall should be reached in ample time to permit of the dog having a rest before he is due to be in the ring, and the time of his appearance before the judge should be carefully noted and rigidly adhered to, for unpunctuality in this respect is the height of discourtesy, besides being unfair to the other dogs who are kept waiting in the unaccustomed atmosphere of the ring. Some judges, unfortunately, are more lenient than others in this matter and permit the entry of the offenders minutes after the stewards have called their numbers.

The ideal handler, as the shrewd observer will note, is on terms of the closest sympathy with his charge. Through the leash lightly but firmly held his delicate finger-tips seem to be communicating his innermost thoughts to the dog. He plays upon the dog's feelings like a master of the violin—but his ultimate aim is to impress the heart and head of the judge whose impartiality is characterized either by a sphinx-like inscrutability of countenance, or by a smile that, like Monna Lisa's, defies analysis. It is not the impression created by the handler himself that counts; no matter how beautiful the crease down his trousers, the judge has eyes only for the legs of the little fellow at the end of the string; the handler may have a Mussolini-like jaw, but what counts is the punishing strength of the same feature in his canine charge. Nevertheless, it is handling that, other things being equal, "gets away with" the awards, and the aspiring exhibitor-handler will not count as time wasted the hours spent in watching the masters of this art. One feels that the cinematograph in its slow-motion form could throw a good deal of light upon an art whose secrets seem to be more elusive than those of a great golfer's swing or a master-batsman's late cut.

There are a number of unwritten laws which the experienced handler observes. If it is necessary to speak to the judge his remarks are concise and to the point, and this also applies to his answers to any questions the judge may ask. Moreover, the good handler cultivates an air of detachment from the lookers-on and refrains from commenting upon the proceedings to those at the ringside while the judge is occupied in his difficult task. And for the sake of good sportsmanship the model handler, if his charge has failed to catch the judge's eye, will not omit to congratulate the successful handler, and in a good-natured way seek to compare notes with those either more or less fortunate than himself.

84

PREPARATION FOR SHOW

Some of the little needs of the show dog are inclined to be overlooked in the hurry and scurry. As a rule the temperature of the hall is high and the dog should be allowed an ample supply of fresh water. Well-cared for dogs are never left unattended on their benches for hours at a stretch. Quite apart from the dog's needs there is the disadvantage of having well-meaning visitors making a fuss of temporarily deserted dogs. In a show it is quite on the cards that one or more of the exhibits is suffering from distemper in its earliest stages and the germ is quite easily carried on the visitor's hand from one dog to another as each is petted in turn. A point to consider when the hour of your dog's entry into the ring approaches, is whether he is likely to be overcome by the excitement of the occasion and so prejudice his chances by boisterousness in the ring. Alertness is a characteristic much to be desired, but if the dog jumps about continually, like a cat on hot bricks, he is hardly likely to find favour with the judges. If the dog's temperament is thoroughly understood the handler will be able to estimate from his mood before entry into the ring whether he is likely to misbehave in this way and will administer a small dose of some sedative previously prescribed by the vet. Food at show-time should be light in character, milk foods forming the staple dish. The average dog gets less exercise at a show than at any other time and a normal diet is consequently liable to upset him. The exhibitor should make sure that everything necessary for grooming, etc. (not forgetting a first-aid outfit in case his own dog, or somebody else's, gets bitten), is packed. Towels should be included, as it is often necessary to exercise a dog in the rain. A useful precaution is to take a padlock and small chain so that one's attaché case or other receptacle for gear may be locked to the bench while one is absent. The exhibitor who wishes to rely upon his dogs receiving certain necessary attentions, such as exercising and watering, can only make certain in one way—by seeing to the dog himself. It is hopeless to place implicit trust in the tender mercies of the show attendants, who are at the beck and call of many people.

The novice exhibitor must also learn the most important lesson of all and one that, even should he forget all the rest, will be accounted to him for righteousness—and that is to accept the judge's verdict with a smile, and to congratulate with all sincerity the more fortunate owner whose dog has gained the day. That is the true essence of sportsmanship, and it makes victory all the sweeter when the pendulum of fortune swings the other way, as it assuredly will. A good loser may not receive one of the prizes, but he wins something of greater value—the respect and admiration of his fellow contestants.

CHAPTER VIII

THE BREEDING OF "WIRES" AND REARING OF PUPPIES

The essentials to success—Luck an important factor—Do not expect to make money—The true spirit of breeding—The specialist Clubs—Willing helpers—How the wise novice begins—Brood bitches and stud-dogs—Prices of brood bitches—The choice of sire—Stud-fees—Complementary qualities—Theories of breeding—Arrangements for service —Transport arrangements—The gestation period—Whelping quarters—Whelping—The arrival of puppies—Checking the progress—The nursing mother—Dew-claws and dock- ing—Weaning—Disposing of puppies—Skin troubles— Feeding—Playthings—The dog newspapers—The fascina- tion of breeding.

THE breeding of any sort of pedigree stock, and especially of dogs, is a venture on which it is rash to prophesy.   Success in dog-breeding, and par- ticularly of " Wires ", calls for an intelligence in the breeder above the average; an inborn *flair* for the job; resourcefulness, and an intuition which less successful competitors in the game would either describe as uncanny or dismiss as showing how extraordinarily lucky some people can be. Luck, it must be admitted, does play a part, and the unlucky breeder (there are people who strike snags at every turn) is unlikely to progress very far. But many of the untoward happenings in dog-breeding could be avoided if only the breeder possesses in sufficient measure the desirable attributes above mentioned, added to a sound knowledge of the general rules of the game. Dog-breeding is, we think, best likened to a game as the term is understood to-day: a deadly seriousness and the elimination, as far as possible, of all hazard; a dignified philosophy in the face of setbacks, and the suppression of undue elation when it is appropriate to pat oneself on the back. The best initial advice to those contemplating the breeding of " Wires " would be the same (but in all seriousness) as that given by Mr. Punch to those about to get married. However, people *will* take up dog-breeding in spite of warnings because they feel they must, and it is unfortunate that this irresistible urge is not confined to those who possess the requisite qualities for success.

There is one paramount piece of advice that should always be given to the would-be breeder of " Wires "' and that is, " Never go into the game in the expectation of making money out of it ". Money has been, is, and will continue to be made in this way; but it is safe to say that when most of the leading " Wire " breeders first succumbed to the charms of the breed, they began operations with little idea of securing any material gain from their hobby. They started in a small way for the pure love of the thing and the later development into a means of making money has been purely incidental. The breeder who is imbued with this, the only true spirit in which the subject should be taken up, to the end of his career places the well-being and improvement of the breed first, and never regards the products of his kennel as so many pieces of merchandise of greater or lesser market value. The " Wire " admirer fired with ambitions to breed, should not only be prepared to adopt the hobby for fun; he must be prepared to lose money. But for the dog-lover who is also in love with dog-breeding the enjoyment derived amply off-sets all but the severest blows of Fate.

The best way to begin is to sit at the feet of the masters. These you will find in the member-ship of the Specialist Clubs, one or more of which every devotee of the breed should join; and you will meet them at all the shows of any consequence where, if you are a good listener, you will find them ready to open their hearts to you, with many living examples of the "Wire" conveniently at hand to point the moral and adorn the tale. Listen to them; make notes while the memory of these pearls of wisdom are still in your mind; for most of these people, while they are ready to talk if encouraged, are not given to shouting their lore of the "Wire" from the house-tops, and you may be the repository of some valuable idea that has not been communicated to another living soul. Thus a capacity to assimilate the fruits of others' years of experience, gained in most instances after many trials and tribulations, is a most valuable one, and may make all the difference between success and failure at the outset. Among the hints acquired in this way you will find many divergences of opinion, and possibly some that contradict each other. But, generally speaking, the earnest seeker after knowledge will be able to recognize the incontrovertible main truths running like a golden thread through the discourses of those who know. For the rest, he must accept or reject as his instinct guides him; at any rate whichever counsel he accepts, even if he has been ill-advised, he will be following in the footsteps of one who has succeeded despite his mistakes. And he will be secure in the knowledge that the " Wire " is one of the " safest " of breeds to take up. Other dogs may have their little boom for a year or two; the " Wire " is one of the few that, year in, year out, pursue the even tenor of their way, which only a cataclysm could disturb.

The wise novice will begin with a first-class brood bitch. He will, unless he has money to " burn ", refrain from considering the purchase of a stud dog. First-flight stud-dogs command fabulous prices, and second or third-class specimens, one feels inclined to say, should be prohibited by law from reproducing their kind. There is a fairly reliable way of determining the breeding qualities of a bitch. If she has already produced some puppies that have won in good company, that is proof of her capacity as a dam. As for her attributes from the show standpoint, she should be of first-class pedigree and approximate in all respects to a good standard, although she may possess some very minor defects which would prejudice her show chances in the very best of company. These defects need not detract from her capacity to produce tip-top puppies, for those slight blemishes can be, and very often are, successfully eliminated from the progeny by the careful selection of a sire whose points are complementary —that is, who excels in those points in which the dam is lacking. It is hopeless to attempt a " dip in the lucky bag " when the purchase of a brood bitch is contemplated, for anything in the nature of a bargain at a knock-out price would inevitably have reached the ears of the *cognoscenti* long before the novice could get a look-in. A bitch of the right class will probably cost £40 or £50— some brood bitches have changed hands at considerably more than double that figure—but you will be building on a sound foundation, and you may go near to recouping yourself on the first litter. Next comes the important question of the choice of sire—and here it is well, when a likely dog comes to notice, to make a few discreet inquiries among the fancy as to whether he is one of the "siring-machine" sort that is literally worked to death to coin money for his owners; or whether the multitudes of bitches that are sent to him for service *are* actually served by him, or by some lesser-known (and less popular) deputy. In either case the kennel would be one to avoid. The stud fee, if the dog of one's choice is a proven begetter of winners, will be in the neighbourhood of five or six guineas. Mention has already been made of the desirability of setting out to balance, in the litter, any weak points in the dam by seeking a sire with a superabundance of those points. This does not apply merely to the physical side, but to the mental as well. A shy bitch should be mated, for preference, to a dog with any amount of "devil"; compensation for a short-headed dam should be sought in a long-headed sire, and so on throughout the whole standard. At any cost avoid a dog that displays one or more of the identical defects possessed by the bitch, for the fault will almost certainly be emphasized by the offspring. Before actually deciding upon a sire, a preliminary study might well be made of one of the popular works upon Mendelism. It is only recently that investigators have begun to explore the value of Mendel's theories in relation to dog-breeding, and it will be interesting to compare your own conclusions, after a study of the scientists' views, with those of the experienced breeders whom you have consulted and who have worked things out in their own way. There are many theories of breeding, other than Mendel's, which have their adherents. Some hold by the theory of the " tail female ", believing that the female's influence on her offspring remains uppermost through each successive generation. Others swear by the figure-breeding system, following the theories of Bruce-Lowe which were first applied to racehorses. Do not delay your search for a suitable sire until the time of the bitch's coming into season is imminent. And before finally deciding it is just as well to ascertain the opinion of the former owner of your bitch on the question whether the blood lines of the prospective sire are likely to coalesce satisfactorily with hers. One important precaution before service is to make sure that the bitch is free from worms.

As is generally known, the bitch has to be sent

to the stud-dog, and all arrangements should be made well in advance. It is always best for the bitch's owner to accompany her to the sire's kennels, unless the latter's owner is a personal friend who can be implicitly trusted to see the mating through in a manner above criticism. The œstrum or season occurs twice a year, and its appearance is characterized by unusual high spirits (especially when in company with other dogs), accompanied by local inflammation and a coloured discharge. This latter is not as profuse in some individuals as in others, and in some is hardly noticeable. The best time for mating is from the ninth to the eleventh day from the commencement of the discharge. Some hold that the timing of the service earlier or later in the course of the œstrum determines which parent's good points shall predominate in the offspring. They argue that if mating is encompassed when the bitch's desire for service has not reached its culmination, or when it is on the wane, the sire's virtues will be uppermost in the offspring. And conversely they maintain that the bitch's qualities will prevail if service is arranged when the œstrum is at its fullest. There is little scientific support for this theory, which is as well, for it would be discouraging to those who arrange a mating on a complementary basis. One reason why it is advisable for the bitch's owner to be present at the service is that the bitch may evince a disinclination to accept the attentions of her suitor which may have to be overcome by persuasion, which she will not tolerate from a stranger. However, if the service is apparently a success it is desirable, after all the trouble that has been taken, to make assurance doubly sure by arranging for a second service two days after the first. But this understanding had best be come to when the initial arrangements are made, as the stud-dog owner is otherwise quite within his rights in permitting one service only for the agreed stud-fee. If her home is a considerable distance away the bitch should be allowed to remain at the stud-dog's kennels for at least two days after service, as otherwise the disturbance of travel may render the service ineffective, and moreover, it renders easier the task of keeping a close watch upon the bitch in case she might accept the attentions of another dog. If

97

G

she is sent by train, one of the specially constructed travelling boxes or baskets should be used.

The normal period of gestation is sixty-two days, but whelping has been known to take place several days earlier or later, and it is advisable to have the whelping quarters prepared in good time and not to defer this until the eleventh hour. After the first two or three days subsequent to mating, the bitch should resume her normal routine and be given just as much exercise as she has previously been accustomed to. Food should be plentiful and varied, and there is no necessity to restrict the amount of exercise until a month has passed. All speculation as to whether the bitch is in whelp or not should normally be determined by the end of the fifth week, although it is by no means rare for the signs to manifest themselves much earlier or later.

The whelping quarters should be arranged to the bitch's obvious liking, and if she appears to dislike them, every endeavour should be made to make her more comfortable. Otherwise she is likely to have her puppies in some highly inconvenient and perhaps inaccessible place that is more to her taste. One can purchase a special whelping-box, but this may be classed as a luxury, and a wooden box of the small packing-case variety, with low sides, will serve equally well. It should be raised slightly from the floor and placed in some warm, draught-proof, and secluded corner. Newspapers form an excellent bedding for the whelping-box, and they should be frequently changed. As the whelping time approaches the bitch will become very uneasy, and if it is likely to be the owner's first experience of a whelping, it is worth while to try to arrange for the presence of a friend to whom this natural wonder is no new thing. He would probably be able to reassure the novice owner who is naturally nervous at such a time, and would quickly recognize any untoward happening which appeared to call for veterinary intervention. Give the expectant mother a mild aperient of olive oil or liquid paraffin when the whelping time is a few days ahead. If the bitch appears to have secreted an ample quantity of milk, meals should be reduced a day or two before whelping, as otherwise an excess of milk may give rise to acidity. As the crucial time becomes a matter of hours, the bitch will probably become excited, and very restless and fussy in the arrangement of her bed. Now is the time to call for the presence of the experienced friend. As the pangs of labour increase the bitch will probably pant a good deal, and warm milk will help to make things easier for her. If she appears to be having an exceptionally rough time a few drops of brandy may be given. When whelping begins the puppies should arrive at intervals of a few minutes, but if there is delay between deliveries every possible assistance should be given—but this, however, does not include the use of instruments. That is a matter exclusively for the vet. should his services become necessary. The normal mother herself severs the umbilical cord and consumes the fœtal envelope, but in some cases—and this is where the advice of the " old hand " is invaluable —it is necessary for the envelope to be broken by human aid, and the umbilical cord similarly tied and severed. In any event the puppies should be handled as little as possible, otherwise they may be eaten by the bitch. When whelping is finished the bitch should be allowed to remain undisturbed for a few hours, with a supply of warm milk within reach. When she has rested, the bedding should be replaced at the earliest opportunity by something softer—a piece of old blanket, folded, is advisable. If there are more puppies than the bitch can manage, the surplus will have to be either placed under a foster-mother, or else humanely disposed of in a bucket of tepid water. In this latter regrettable alternative the choice should be made with extreme care.

A reliable method of checking the progress of puppies from birth is to weigh them the day after birth, and thereafter keep a weekly record of weight on a chart. During the first few days after whelping, the nursing mother should be given one of the proprietary milk foods as a staple item in a light diet. The puppies' dew-claws should be removed before they are a fortnight old and their tails docked. The amount of the tail taken away is approximately one-third; the ultimate ideal to aim at is that when the dog is full-grown an imaginary horizontal line resting on the highest point of the ears, and carried to the tail shall also rest on the tip of that member when held at the

correct angle.   Within a week after the birth of
the puppies the mother should have been allowed
gradually to resume her normal diet with the extra
rations, particularly of milk and meat, necessary
to nourish her voracious family.   The gift of sight
will come to the puppies when they are between
two and three weeks' old, and at the fourth week
the very gradual process of weaning should begin
by dipping the puppies' noses in a saucer of warm
goat's or cow's milk.   If they seem slow in the
uptake they can be encouraged to acquire the
flavour by being spoon-fed.   This will relieve the
mother a little from their importunities, and a
further relief can be arranged for her by placing
a stool or box near the family nest, to which she
can retire when so disposed, out of reach of the
puppies.   The puppies should be completely
weaned at eight weeks, and the earliest opportunity
should be taken to dispose of the least likely of
the puppies for what they will fetch, for, after
weaning, the presumed second-raters are just a
drain on the resources, as they eat just as much as
the puppies for whom you hope to get good prices.
There should be no difficulty in disposing of them

among the legion of "Wire" admirers who have probably never seen a dog show and never want to. It may be, of course, that one of these puppies will be acquired by some far-seeing or unusually lucky fancier, and will develop into the best dog of the litter. But that is a remote possibility, and the philosophic breeder would not begrudge anyone this piece of good fortune which would, after all, add lustre to the breeder's name as well as the owner's. The litter should be carefully watched from birth for any signs of skin trouble, as puppies of all breeds are liable to contract eczema, which may prove very difficult to cure unless taken in hand early. Fleas and other vermin should also be dealt with promptly by sprinkling disinfectants of a non-carbolic nature on the bedding. The puppies' coats can also be given a dusting of some insecticide that will not harm the skin. As the puppies grow more vigorous and playful it is as well to provide them with playthings, such as hard indiarubber balls (of a size too big to be swallowed) and indiarubber "bones", which are preferable to natural ones. To expedite the process of disposing of the litter, the columns of the dog newspapers are a good medium, but always make use of the " deposit and approval " method with prospective purchasers living at a distance, as the shady dealers have to acquire their stock from somewhere, and a breeder with an unfamiliar name is sometimes marked down as a likely victim. The puppies should be assessed at reasonable prices (if possible after consultation with an un-biased but knowledgeable friend), and it is best not to tolerate haggling on the part of a prospective purchaser. You will probably want to keep at least one puppy with the idea of showing him or her later. It is probably better to keep two, not only because one would be lonely, but because it will be much more satisfactory later on, to have a choice for show purposes.

If Fortune has not been too unkind, the first essay in breeding will be but the forerunner of many others. There is a great deal to learn about the breeding of " Wires " before the breeder can congratulate himself that he knows half as much as some who have spent a long lifetime in the game. Such aspects as in-breeding with all its surprises (pleasant and otherwise), the union of blood-lines that may or may not mix, will repay all the study that the newcomer finds himself able to give. But if the science of dog-breeding were a simple matter its fascination would be gone, for perfect "Wires" would be as common as mass-production motor-cars.

CHAPTER IX

FEEDING; TREATMENT FOR AILMENTS

Proprietary foods—Flesh foods and biscuits—Liver—How to test biscuit foods—Variety in diet—The superstition about milk—Wholemeal bread—Quantities—Vegetables—Orange or tomato juice—Drinking water.

(i) HINTS ON FEEDING

THE number of proprietary foods for dogs has increased amazingly during the past few years, and most of these foods appear to conform to every standard of purity, although the quality is not yet regulated by law as is that of foodstuffs for cattle. It is claimed for some dog foods in which cereals form the main constituent that they are a complete food in themselves, but in the writer's opinion such a claim is an exaggeration. The natural food of a dog is flesh, and every dog's dietary should contain a fair proportion of meat. It is difficult to lay down hard and fast rules as to the quantity of meat to be given, or whether it should be cooked or raw. In any event, any meat which gives rise to the slightest suspicion as to its freshness should be rejected, and liver and other portions of the viscera should never be fed raw because of the danger of tapeworm. Some owners hold that meat should represent three-quarters of a dog's diet, and biscuit the remainder, but this rests a good deal with the individual dog's idiosyncrasies.

It is a mistake with biscuit-foods to purchase quantities that will last for a long period. It is best to purchase just sufficient to last for a week, and to test each batch for freshness. There is a crisp feel and a wholesome smell about biscuit foods in good condition, and any that smell musty or otherwise disagreeable should be rejected. Cereal foods should be kept in tins or earthenware jars in a dry place. " Wires ", like most other breeds, enjoy variety in diet. There is a super-stition that milk foods given to young puppies produce worms. This is nonsense and the puppy who is denied milk is liable to contract rickets and suffer other serious consequences of malnutrition. Stale wholemeal bread moistened—but not soaked to the point of sloppiness—is good for dogs of all ages. As regards quantity the average grown dog will need on an average from half to three-quarters of a pound of meat a day with a few ounces of meal, biscuit or stale brown bread.

Potatoes should never be given and green vegetables only occasionally. Orange or tomato juice is valuable, although some dogs require a good deal of persuasion in taking these. Plenty of clean, fresh water in clean vessels should be accessible to the dogs at all times, except when they are over-heated. Incidentally, the depositing of a lump of rock sulphur in the drinking water is quite useless, for rock sulphur is absolutely insoluble in water.

(ii) TREATMENT FOR AILMENTS

The following remarks are intended for the owner's guidance in treating minor ailments which do not appear to call for a veterinary surgeon's intervention. More serious disorders are also referred to, in order that the owner may be able to recognize the symptoms at an early age. In all serious cases the services of a veterinary surgeon should be obtained as soon as possible; where palliatives for major ailments are mentioned in this chapter they are given so that the owner may administer temporary relief pending the arrival of the vet. Diagnosis by an amateur is not always accurate, and the more serious disorders of dogs, as of human beings, should always receive the attention of a skilled practitioner.

Abscesses are due to a bacterial infection.   In addition to local inflammation and swelling there is sometimes fever and other constitutional disturbances.   Relief is obtained by fomentations, which encourage supperation.   Care should be taken not to apply the fomentations too hot; they should be just bearable on the back of the hand. When the abscess comes to a head it should be painted with iodine, lanced with a sharp, sterilized knife, gently squeezed, and then bathed with a mild antiseptic such as a weak solution of hydrogen peroxide, and kept open to permit of drainage for a few days until it is clean.   Abscesses in the throat or near vital organs call for careful treatment by a vet.

Anal Abscess is usually due to feeding errors. There is usually much pain and irritation and the dog drags himself along the ground in a sitting posture.   The abscess must be lanced, and an antiseptic ointment applied.   The bowels require careful regulation, and oily laxatives, such as medicinal paraffin are best when this condition is present.

Asthma. An affection which mainly attacks dogs out of condition, or those not given sufficient exercise. There is difficulty in breathing and the bark is husky, the trouble being due to a spasmodic contraction in the bronchial tubes. There is no cure for asthma, but relief can often be given by careful regulation of the dog's diet and habits. The dog should be given as much exercise as possible and dry foods are, in the main, preferable for the canine victims of asthma.

Bites, Snake. There is always the risk of snake-bite where the solitary British poisonous snake, the adder, is found. A ligature should be tied above the wound when it is on a limb, and the wound should be opened to permit of free bleeding. Permanganate of potash in dry form or peroxide of hydrogen should then be applied.

Bronchitis begins, like many respiratory diseases, with a cold, accompanied by cough and difficulty in breathing. The nose and mouth are hot and dry and the eyes red and inflamed. The dog should be kept in a warm and even temperature, but not too dry an atmosphere. Hot poultices should be applied to the dog's chest, and internal treatment should consist of careful doses of paragoric cough mixture three times a day. As bronchitis may develop into something more serious, the vet. should be summoned.

Canker of the Ear in its dry form is due to a parasite, and there is considerable pain which the dog seeks to alleviate by scratching the ear with his paw. The first object of treatment is to eliminate the parasite responsible. The entrance to the ear should be thoroughly cleansed with a weak solution of hydrogen peroxide, and the ear cavity syringed with the same mixture. Afterwards nitrate of mercury ointment should be carefully worked into the ear.

Wet Canker. With wet canker there is considerable discharge. Small quantities of lead lotion should be poured into the ear twice a day, and zinc ointment worked into the ear as in the dry form. The dog's general health should be given careful attention.

Colds of the common variety are often contracted by dogs. As they lead sometimes to worse complaints they call for prompt attention. Most of the symptoms are the same as in human beings —sneezing, shivering, temperature above normal, with watering of the eyes and sometimes excessive thirst, and a disinclination for exercise. Keep the patient in an even temperature for a day or two after the symptoms have abated, and feed on a light diet.

Colic is characterized by severe abdominal pain which causes the dog to howl and arch his back. Sometimes it is caused by an internal chill, or else some dietary disturbance. Chlorodyne in tiny doses is often efficacious, but persistent trouble of this kind should always be dealt with by a vet.

Constipation is, as a rule, due either to lack of exercise, insufficient " roughage " to induce a natural motion of the bowels, or to otherwise unsuitable diet. Raw meat and liver (the latter cooked) have mildly laxative properties, and in the summer the dog should be given in his first drinking-water in the morning, as much Glauber or Epsom Salts as will go on a sixpence. As lubricants, medicinal paraffin or olive oil are excellent, and the latter may be given with food.

Coughs may be due to the presence of a bone or other foreign body in the throat, or symptomatic of a variety of ailments mainly of the respiratory organs, but sometimes are a prelude to distemper. If the trouble is serious the dog will soon go off his food, but if he remains otherwise normal after a day or so, he should be examined for throat obstruction.

Diarrhœa is just as often a symptom of something else as of a passing derangement of the stomach. It often occurs in young puppies when they are introduced to a solid diet, and in older dogs it is frequently induced by a change of food, the eating of something tainted or sour, or a dietary containing too much vegetable food. Administer a mild dose of caster oil at the onset, and keep the dog on a light diet in an even temperature until the symptoms have subsided, in case the trouble may be the initial stage of some major ailment. If the trouble fails to clear up quickly a vet. should be consulted.

Distemper. The scourge of the canine race is not the inevitable lot of every dog. Some go through a long life unscathed, while others, despite popular belief to the contrary, have more than one attack. Recent researches into the disease have resulted in the production of substances which are claimed, with strong supporting evidence, almost infallibly to prevent or (less infallibly) to cure the disease. Every dog-lover will hope that as time goes on these claims will be substantiated. In the opinion of many people who have devoted a life-time to dogs, the surest preventive is to keep the dog absolutely up to concert pitch with ample exercise, careful grooming, a properly balanced diet, first-class housing and protection from damp. The investigations of the distemper problem discerned many points of resemblance to human influenza, and it seems possible that the two diseases are related, although there is no evidence whatever that persons in contact with cases of canine distemper are more liable to influenza, or *vice versa.* In fact, during a recent influenza epidemic, enquiries showed that the number of cases of distemper among dogs was below the normal for the particular time of year. However, it is as well to be able to recognize the symptoms. The dog becomes listless and dull-eyed, with a hot and dry nose and a distaste for food. He may, or may not have a cough, but don't wait for this symptom before suspecting distemper and calling the vet. Within two or three days the eyes and nose develop a watery discharge and the eyelids often become inflamed and swollen. The patient should be completely isolated from other dogs and kept in a dry and draught-proof place which can be kept at a steady temperature of about 68°. An invalid diet, should be given— meat extracts, calf's foot jelly, beef tea, beef extracts and the light milk foods. The eyes and nose should be regularly cleansed of the discharge and afterwards smeared gently with a little vaseline. The teeth should be kept clean to obviate corrosion. On no account if the dog's life is valued should the amateur attempt to see the dog through distemper without veterinary advice. So many complications and tragic sequelæ are due to the failure of the untrained eye to observe symptoms and developments that would have been promptly diagnosed by the trained man. Convalescence from distemper is somewhat pro-tracted, as there is always danger of relapse if the dog reverts to normal routine too quickly. The return to more solid food should be done gradually, beginning with steamed fish, milk puddings, and later on a little minced meat. The dog should continue to be kept in the same warm situation until the expiry of three weeks after his temperature has become normal. Exercise also should be gradually increased daily from the minimum until the dog has fully recovered his strength.

Eye Troubles in dogs are of various kinds. One of the commonest is conjunctivitis, which is an inflamation of the conjunctivæ or mucous membrane of the eye and may be induced by the entry of foreign bodies, such as dirt or grit. The sufferer should be kept in a subdued light and the eyes irrigated with boracic lotion. Each night the eyelids should be anointed with yellow oxide of mercury ointment as otherwise there will be a tendency for them to stick. Severe attacks of conjunctivitis call for veterinary intervention.

A frequent aftermath of distemper is the appearance of white spots on the eyeballs. They will, as a rule, gradually disappear of themselves, but their departure may be hastened and the eyes strengthened by regularly bathing the eyes with warm boracic lotion.

Eczema is a skin affliction which is more prevalent during summer than winter. It is the safest plan when eczema is suspected to obtain veterinary diagnosis as there is a similarity between a number of skin diseases which often renders them undistinguishable to the untrained eye. The cause is usually some digestive disturbance arising through an unsuitable or badly adjusted dietary, or through worms. In either case the condition calls first for internal treatment without which it is impossible for the skin condition to clear up. Gentle aperients and a soothing lotion are almost invariably prescribed for eczema.

Fits are varied both in nature and cause. Many dogs are subject to epileptic fits. In these the victim is seized with violent spasms and almost at once becomes unconscious. There is often loss of control of the excretory organs and foaming at the mouth. As there is also a danger of the dog biting his tongue very severely, a piece of wood should, if possible be placed between the jaws.

The spasmodic phase is normally succeeded by a period of quiet during which the dog is unconscious, and this is followed by further spasms before consciousness returns. At the onset steps should be taken to restrain the dog from running away, and cold water poured on the head is the best restorative. The vet. should be consulted.

Foot Troubles are mainly accidental, although interdigital cysts, which arise from some constitutional disturbances, are perhaps the commonest of all foot ailments. Some hold the theory that dogs exercised on grass-land are more subject to cysts, but they are very common among town-dwelling dogs. The dog becomes lame and licks the affected paws. They should be protected by chamois-leather boots, and poulticed regularly until ready for lancing, and then thoroughly emptied and bathed with boracic lotion. Internally, calcium lactate may be administered under veterinary advice.

Irritation is often set up in a dog's feet by soft tar picked up on the roads. The tar can be removed with a little fresh butter, or olive oil, and the inflammation allayed by bathing the affected feet for a few minutes twice a day in a solution of methylated spirit—one part to four of water. Long claws should be clipped and any cracks made smooth with a fine file. Contused pads should be bathed with boracic lotion and bruises painted with compound tincture of benzoin. Dew-claws should have been removed in early puppyhood as they are liable to become torn.

Gastritis is often caused by a chill. Drinking cold water when over-heated is one of the commonest ways in which this trouble is set up. There is excessive thirst, sickness and diarrhœa and a desire on the part of the dog to seek out the coolest possible place in which to lie. Solid foods must be withheld and the dog given just barley water or soda water, with or without milk. As a sedative carbonate of bismuth should be given. A veterinary surgeon should be called if the vomiting and diarrhœa have not abated within twenty-four hours.

Hysteria has been ascribed to many causes and is still as provocative of argument as ever. The only definite result of the investigations so far appears to be that certain types of food formerly suspect have been absolved from blame. One opinion is that the disease is due to an aural parasite, but the suspected organism has not yet been identified. There seems to be good ground for the view held by some that the trouble is contagious, for it will sometimes sweep through a kennel, leaving none of the canine occupants unscathed. This is not definite proof of contagion however, and there is much support for the contention that successive cases in the same kennel are due to the effect of suggestion by the first dog so attacked. At any rate, the symptoms are unmistakeable. The victim dashes about oblivious of any object in his path, and appears to be possessed by a terror of some unseen thing. There is always the danger of injury by striking objects in his headlong rushes, and steps to restrain him should at once be taken and a sedative administered. He should be kept as quiet as possible and in a subdued light until the symptoms have subsided. Whatever his diet, a change should be made and mild aperients administered.

Jaundice—the yellow variety—sometimes arises through drinking excessive quantities of cold water when over-heated. Rats are said to be carriers of the disease in kennels and sometimes the cause is an obstruction of the bile duct by a gallstone. The symptoms are a yellowish tinge of the eyes and skin with high temperature and staring coat. Jaundice demands skilled attention, and the vet. should be called as soon as the symptoms develop. The more serious form of jaundice is very sudden in onset. The eyes and skin do not become yellow but there are many distressing symptoms including fever, vomiting and diarrhœa.

The dog rarely recovers from that form of jaundice, which usually proves fatal in a few hours.

Mange manifests itself in two forms—sarcoptic and follicular. Sarcoptic mange is the commoner form and is more easily curable than the follicular variety. The trouble is sometimes very difficult to diagnose and veterinarians are not always sure until they have made a microscopic examination. There is considerable irritation with either kind. Both are parasitic, and in the more serious follicular variety the itching is intense. Contrary to widely-held opinion, mange in a dog is no reflection upon his owner. In any case it is a vet's. job to diagnose the trouble and prescribe a course of treatment. Above all, don't experiment with cure-alls or much-advertised specifics. Where these quackeries appear to have succeeded the dog has probably got well in spite of their use. With follicular mange the mortality rate is very high.

Poisoning. The commonest form of malicious poisoning is by strychnine placed on pieces of meat. There is violent contortion of the body accompanied by muscular stiffness. An emetic should at once be administered, the most suitable being a strong solution of salt and warm water. As an antidote give olive oil or brandy and apply hot-water bottles to stomach and back. The vet. should, of course, be immediately summoned. A good deal of " accidental " poisoning occurs during " rat-weeks " and at other times through the laying of baits for vermin without taking the steps required by law to prevent access by domestic animals. Where phosphorus has been used the symptoms are vomiting of blood, abdominal distension and intense thirst. As an emetic give 5 grs. of copper sulphate in solution in warm water, followed, as an antidote, by frequent administration of a weak solution of permanganate of potash. Oily substances should *not* be given in cases of phosphorus poisoning. Carbolic acid poisoning is caused sometimes by the use of soaps or disinfectants containing this substance, which is highly dangerous to dogs. The chief symptoms are diarrhœa, shivering and collapse. Give olive oil or brandy while awaiting the vet's. arrival, and keep the dog warm with hot water bottles and rugs.

Rabies is now, to all intents and purposes, non-existent in this country, although one would imagine, from the symptoms and warnings which appear on every dog-licence that it was still of common occurrence. The rigid imposition of quarantine upon imported dogs has stamped out the disease, although cases occur often on the Continent, and in the East many people die every year from the bites of rabid dogs.

Rheumatism is induced by damp and cold and may take either an acute or chronic form. The bowels should be regularized with Epsom or Glauber Salts, and a mild embrocation repeatedly rubbed into the affected parts. Aspirin often works wonders, and a 5-grain tablet may be given thrice daily. Soft water should be given in preference to the ordinary tap water. In fact, it is worth while always to give dogs of mature age soft water, whether they are rheumatic subjects or not. The chronic form is milder in character than the acute type, being more insidious in onset and progress and less painful. Rheumatic dogs should always be kept dry and warm.

Rickets mainly affects puppies and young dogs and the root cause is a deficiency of Vitamin D in the diet, and/or lack of sunshine and exercise. The joints become enlarged—particularly the knees, hocks and stifles—the ankles are weak, and there is a tendency to become cow-hocked. Anæmia is also a frequent symptom. Give mineral tonics and bone-forming preparations of which any chemists will recommend a selection. A table-spoonful of cod-liver oil emulsion twice daily is also beneficial. Milk puddings and other foods containing milk are helpful.

Ringworm is an easily identifiable disease characterized by circular patches on the skin of a scaly nature. The adjacent hair is harsh and dry, and comes away easily. The affected parts should be washed with soap and warm water to remove the scales, and paint with tincture of iodine. Where the scales cannot be easily removed they should be softened with olive oil. The process should be repeated on alternate days. Applications of salicylic ointment after cleansing are often beneficial.

Warts often appear on the eyelids, ears, mouth and lips, but other parts of the body, especially in dogs of advanced years, are not invulnerable. Warts should never be cut, as this causes them to spread. A single wart can often be treated—if conveniently situated—by tying a piece of silk around its neck, causing it eventually to drop off. Warts on the mouth and lips should be treated with a salicylic acid solution, or one consisting of a tablespoonful of common soda in half-a-pint of water. In obstinate cases operative treatment is sometimes called for.

Worms are an affliction from which dogs of all ages suffer. Round-worms and tape-worms are the two principal kinds, and both are parasitic in origin and usually contracted through eating raw flesh or other food containing the parasites or their eggs. Puppies commonly suffer from round-worms and the symptoms are almost complete loss of appetite or, alternatively, an enormous capacity for eating, restlessness, bad breath, vomiting, etc. With round-worms evidence of their presence is to be found in the dog's motions or clinging round the anus, and worm medicines should not be given unless these symptoms are present. Medicinal paraffin in small doses may be given on alternate days and if the condition does not clear up within a week or ten days, veterinary advice should be sought. Proprietary vermifuges should be avoided except when prescribed. It is most important when giving worm-medicines that the dose should be carefully adjusted to the individual's special requirements.

Tape-worm is usually revealed by the passage of segments of the worm. Other symptoms are loss of appetite, tightness of the skin, and sometimes diarrhœa. The worm segments evacuated should be burnt. The object of treatment for tape-worm is to compel the head of the parasite, which is attached to the dog's intestine, to relax its hold, and a necessary preliminary is that the dog shall fast for twenty-four hours. One of the best drugs for the purpose is tenalin, which should only be given under veterinary supervision as the dosage calls for most careful calculation according to the dog's size, age and condition. As a rule the tenalin is followed after half-an-hour's interval by a teaspoonful of medicinal paraffin.

Wounds, Burns and Scalds. Wounds call for prompt first-aid treatment pending the arrival of a vet. Where hæmorrhage is profuse it should be checked as quickly as possible by the application of sterile swabs and should then be sterilized by painting with iodine. The surrounding hair should be cut short with scissors. Superficial wounds should be dressed with dry boracic powder after being thoroughly cleansed with a mild antiseptic (not carbolic). Severance of an artery is characterized by the blood flowing in spurts, and a tourniquet should, where practicable, as on a limb, be applied immediately above the wound. In other parts of the body the flow of blood should be staunched by plugs of cotton wool kept in place by pressure or bandages.

Burns and scalds should be treated by cutting away the hair from the affected part and applying picric acid, which is very soothing. If a further application is necessary the part should first be cleansed with a solution of peroxide of hydrogen.

CHAPTER X

HOW TO START A KENNEL

Brood bitches—Fame—Qualities needed for success—Large kennels—The small breeder—The housing question—Breeding material—Brick or wood ?—Flooring—Outdoor runs—Grass *v.* concrete—Portable and sectional kennels—Wire runs—Light, ventilation and warmth—Kennel-maids and kennel-men—The £ s. d. of shows—The compensations of owning a kennel.

IN a previous chapter it has been suggested that as a foundation for a kennel it is far better to invest in a first-class brood bitch, for the stud-dog really worth acquiring would cost a fabulous sum. The present remarks, therefore, are mainly addressed to the breeder who has passed through his novitiate and has begun to feel his feet. He has reared a promising litter or two, possibly with no more ambitious accommodation and fitments for " Wire " breeding than are to be found in the average modest house and garden. He has bred or acquired two or three brood bitches and a promising stud-dog. And now, having been really and truly fallen in love with the breed, he dreams dreams. In fancy he sees his name on a flaming head-line in one of the dog newspapers during big show time: " Mr. Blank's ' Wires ' Sweep The Board ". Perhaps he even imagines himself as reaching the topmost pinnacle of all— a caricature of himself with large head and little body (proof, we suppose, that brains will out) adorning one of these widely-read journals. It is a laudable, and not a vaulting, ambition and there is no reason why with ordinary luck, plus ultra-keenness, a high degree of concentration and an everlasting willingness to learn from others, these lofty eminences should not be attained. But when the decision has been made to take up " Wire " breeding on a larger scale it is still wise to regard it as an interesting hobby and not to build high expectations of making money. If real success is eventually won, the money will come, but blessed is the man or woman who can for ever regard with indifference the reaping of financial benefit and keep uppermost the well-being of his or her dogs. It is fairly safe to assume that, given a fair measure of the qualities mentioned, a moderate degree of success is practically assured. Experts there are who hold that the large kennel is an excrescence, as the dogs therein do not live the normal lives that a friendly, domesticated dog should do. But it is usually from the bigger kennels that the " stars " blaze forth, for the man who does not confine his breeding operations to one brood bitch is likely, if he is a keen student, to probe the secrets of success in less time than the little man. To say this is not to decry the one-dog breeder's efforts, for the fancy would be much the poorer without him.

Apart from the stock the most important matter to consider in founding a kennel is that of housing. If there is any choice, the breeder should select a dry situation and, if circumstances will permit, in a locality where winters are not too severe. For kennel buildings a southern aspect is best, and the choice of building material lies as a rule between brick and wood. Brick is more hygienic, fire-proof and permanent, but wood has in its favour the virtues of comparative cheapness, superior warmth and transportability in the event of a move having to be made. For flooring the best material is concrete, with proper drainage channels and soak-aways. It is the best all-round surface for outdoor runs also. A patch of grass has its uses in dry weather, but there are not a great many days in the year when it is fit for exercising dogs and particularly puppies. So that if, for reasons of space, a choice must be made between grass and concrete runs, the latter should certainly be laid. A total thickness of three inches of concrete is ample and the builder should be asked to finish the surface with a wooden " float ", as this is far less slippery than an ultra-smooth surface, although just as easily cleaned. The makers of portable buildings who exhibit at the dog-shows can supply excellent wooden kennels, both self-contained and sectional, and it is as well to study their structures and prices in order to compare with any estimates which you may wish to obtain for the work to be done locally. The wire runs themselves are extremely important; they must be strong enough and high enough to frustrate the determined efforts of a bitch in season to escape. Wire netting should be of the chain-link variety and preferably of British origin. Some makers guarantee the galvanized coating against cracking for a long period, and it is really worth while spending a little more money on the best wire, as it looks better and lasts many times longer than the cheap makes. Often it is possible to adapt structures built for other purposes, and these are sometimes, by reason of their loftiness, rather more suitable than a specially-built structure would be—unless building costs are a secondary consideration. The main points about kennel buildings, however, whether expressly constructed or otherwise, is that they shall admit ample daylight and sunlight, be well ventilated yet draught-proof, damp-proof and capable of being kept at an evenly warm temperature; easily cleaned and—as far as possible—sound-proof, particularly if the kennels are adjacent to other people's houses. Incidentally, in the case of wooden erections the parts that are vulnerable to dogs' teeth—such as the corners of doors, fencing posts, etc., should be protected either by enamelled iron plates or a lining of wire netting to discourage attempts at escapes by bitches and dogs so minded.

Where stud-dogs are kept it is imperative to have roomy and comfortable accommodation set apart for visiting bitches. For an establishment of any considerable size outside assistance will be necessary in the shape of either a part-time or whole-time kennel-man or kennel-maid. Otherwise the business of looking after the dogs properly is an unremitting tie and a tremendous strain. A girl or youth who is really keen on dogs can assume many of the minor responsibilities, especially if the kennel is represented at shows, and thus leave the owner free to tackle with an easy mind the more important problems and negotiations inseparable from the running of a fair-sized establishment. In these days there are many well-educated youths and girls ready to accept at a nominal salary positions in reputable kennels. There are so many ways in which a keen learner can help that it is a false economy to attempt to do without if there is more than enough for one pair of hands to do comfortably. And many are the emergencies that arise in the business or hobby of breeding when the owner will thank his lucky stars for the presence of somebody else who knows something about the job and will not become panicky.

As for showing, this side of the work of a kennel seldom of itself shows a profit. Prizes worth, say, five or ten pounds may be picked up at a show and the expenses, especially, if the show be a distant one, may run into as much or more. For credits in the ledger one must look to the increased stud fees brought in by those magic oblongs of paste-board decorating the back of the show-bench; and by the enhanced prices of puppies from a winning bitch's subsequent litters.

However, for dog-lovers of a philosophic nature the foundation of a kennel of " Wires " is a red-letter day in their lives. It probably heralds the beginning of a host of little troubles, but it also as a rule has its frequent spells of great joy and supreme satisfaction; and the verdict of every breeder who has known and loved, rejoiced with and suffered for the " Wire " over a long period of years, is that could they live their lives over again their choice would be the same.

INDEX

INDEX

Printed in the United Kingdom
by Lightning Source UK Ltd.
133636UK00001B/47/A